Chakras
for the
21st Century

What Karmic Lessons are you holding in your Chakras?

Claire East

COBOLT
CONNECTION
PUBLISHING

Published by: Cobolt Connection Publishing
Suite 1102, 1 Queens Road,
Melbourne, Victoria 3004, Australia
Email: info@cobolt.com.au

First published 2004

National Library of Australia Cataloguing-in-Publication data:

       East, Claire.
       Chakras for the 21st century : what karmic lessons
       are you holding in your chakras?

       ISBN 0 9752204 4 6

       1. Chakras. 2. Yoga. 3. Theosophy. 4. Spiritual life. I. Title.

       131

Typesetting by: Alphabet Typesetting Pty Ltd
Printed by: C&C Offset Printing Co., Ltd, China
Illustrations: Ross P. Cleland
Illustrations copyright Cobolt Connection P/L 2004

EXPRESSIONS OF GRATITUDE

This book is the outcome of many who came with me on a journey - to all those who participated in the adventure I thank you.

In particular, I would express my gratitude to those students who have completed the Chakra Course with me - I honour you.

I would also like to thank Margaret Elizabeth Atkinson for editing the manuscript, and Ross Cleland for the illustrations, both executing their craft so well.

To all those who dare to see beyond.

DEDICATION:

To all those on a journey; for your courage and willingness.

This book is dedicated to Itzik Ian Moore - a jewel in Yama's crown.

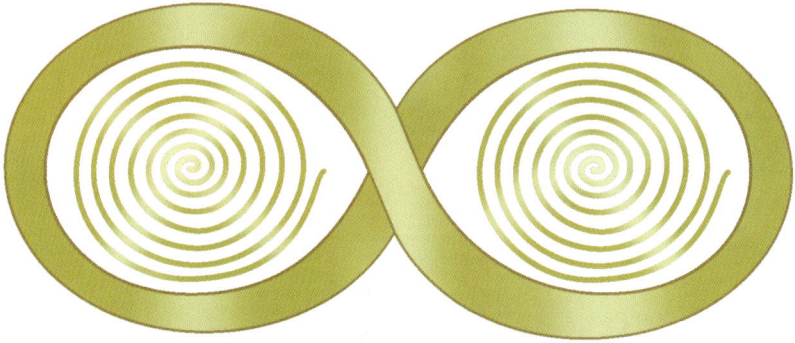

CONTENTS

PREFACE

There are already very many excellent books written about the chakras, that cover many different aspects and dimensions of these amazing energy centres. So why did I write this book?

While working for many years with my clients, teaching the development of chakras, I noticed that their greatest transformation came from being able to heal and bring into balance a blocked or unopened chakra. In order to achieve this permanent change in the functioning of the chakra, the person had to deal with the underlying pattern that had caused the malfunctioning of the chakra in the first place.

Much of the chakra wounding is brought into this life by the soul, to promote healing or transformation. When there is wounding or non-functioning or malfunctioning of a particular chakra, this does not just disappear when you pass over to the spirit world: your soul takes your etheric and astral bodies with it, and these are held for you until you are born again into the flesh. In doing this, our soul ensures that we have another opportunity to bring ourselves into wholeness, purity and joy.

In this book, I have chosen to highlight for you the common underlying patterns associated with each chakra, as I have observed them in my clients over the years.

When you recognize and become aware of the patterns that you may have brought into this life with you, you gain an opportunity to balance the karmic (past) pattern that may be holding you back now.

I have written this book to be a practical key for you to your future.

Blessings and good luck!

Claire East
Melbourne, Australia

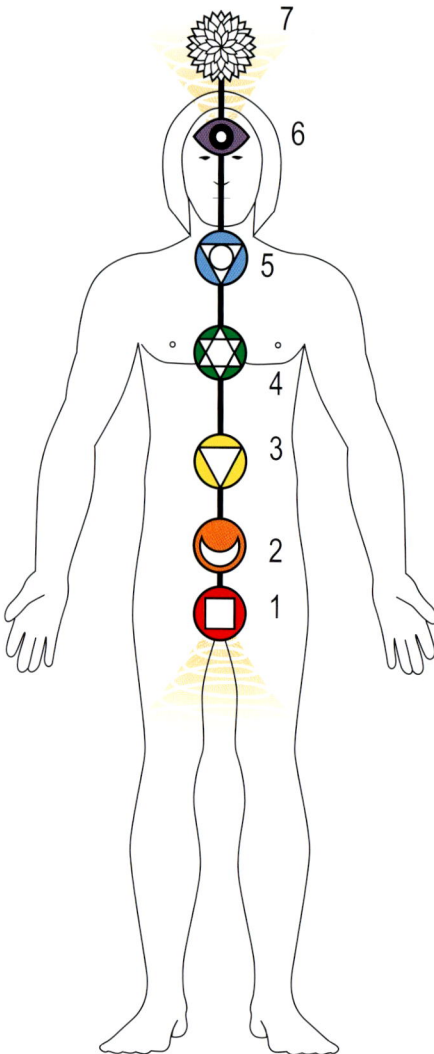

7

6

5

7. Crown Chakra

6. Third Eye Chakra

5. Throat Chakra

4

4. Heart Chakra

3

3. Solar Plexus Chakra

2

2. Sacral Chakra

1

1. Base Chakra

Chakra shown on physical body

INTRODUCTION

Chakra is a sanskrit word meaning 'wheel' or 'circle'. Each chakra is an energy centre, a vortex that draws spiritual energy into our self. Chakras are spiritual centres of light held within our energy field, within our aura. There are seven main chakras in our aura - and the harmonious use of each chakra is essential to our well being, and our wholeness.

Each of the seven main chakras is located near major endocrine organs in the physical body; that is, they are associated with the functioning of the endocrine (hormonal) system in the body. They form etheric centres in the aura, being responsible for processing the spiritual energy into usable energy for the physical body. That is, they "step down" the energy from very high fine vibrations to lower vibrations that can be used by the denser physical body.

In this book we will look at each of the main chakras in turn. You will discover which ones in you need the most work or cleansing, how they work, and what you need in order to bring them into a state of balance.

The chakras are fundamental to your healing, so you will gain a better understanding of the illnesses or states of imbalance that manifest in your life.

*Imbalances need to be corrected at the deepest, 'essential' level, by your self: self-healing is the most empowering and the most deeply transformative of healing methods. It can be helpful to consult others for healing or chakra balancing, for example, but if you do not **change the underlying pattern that caused the dysfunction in the first place then the chakra will go out of balance again.***

This knowledge has been in common use in Eastern cultures for thousands of years, but it is only in the last hundred years or so that this knowledge has become available in the West, introduced by various pioneers, like C.W. Leadbeater, Madame Blavatsky (Theosophy) and Annie Besant.

Humanity is moving towards a greater understanding of the energetic anatomy. This movement can be seen happening in many cultures, and more esoteric knowledge is becoming readily accessible. Look at how common yoga classes are now, meditation, tai chi and so on, which all touch on the energetic aspects of life. We've all heard of them now; the words "chakra" and "kundalini" are also becoming familiar to the collective awareness, and will become much more so in the near future.

Chakras are like flowers (likened to the lotus or rose) that slowly unfurl when they are ready. Like any tender flower each chakra needs the right conditions to open and flourish; again like the flower each chakra needs nurturing and is damaged if mistreated.

Different chakras spin in different directions (you can use a pendulum* to test yours if you like); their movement can be very slow and underactive, or fast and hyperactive, or anything in between. The most important thing is to release blockages and cleanse the chakras, as the body wisdom will correct the spinning as necessary and when ready.

The chakras may be free and open, or closed down or partially open, clogged, torn, unbalanced, off-centre, open in front, closed at the back, muddy or weak in colour and so on.. All these conditions can be balanced by the simple but effective tools which are described for each chakra in this book.

Some methods will work most readily for some people, others will find that other suggestions are more useful to them - we are all different, and you will respond to each remedy according to your own soul vibration.

---

* Hold the pendulum over the point of each chakra and let the pendulum move as it wants to: it will follow the energy and direction of the chakra, and according to the strength of the chakra. It is easier to have a friend use the pendulum for you, while you are laying down.

It is important to note that no one chakra is any more or less important than another. Often people devoted to the spiritual path draw their energy into the upper chakras, believing them to be more important. This behaviour is usually unconscious - whatever we focus our attention on is where our energy goes, so we may draw our energy into our head by thinking too much, or by concentrating on spirituality and ignoring the physical. Balance is the key to a good life!

The lower three chakras need to be open and functioning to some degree for the upper chakras to function - the lower three chakras, that is, the base, sacral and solar plexus, are the foundation for the possibility of a higher consciousness. I can't emphasize enough the importance of the lower three chakras, they need to be strong and functioning well for you to enjoy life here on earth. It is not helpful to deny the aspects of life and self that are associated with the lower chakras.

When functioning well, each chakra draws energy from the atmosphere into itself. This energy may be called prana; simply, prana is a divine energy that is contained within our atmosphere. Each of your spinning centres, the chakras, spins and vibrates at a different frequency, which gives each one a different colour vibration and of course, different functions. The chakra then 'converts' the pranic energy it receives by filtering it through its own lens, so to speak, so that the pranic energy becomes useful for the wellbeing of you and your body. This process is not unlike the way we take food into our physical system, and the food is transformed into something useful for our body, without any conscious effort on our part.

EXERCISE:

For a moment, close eyes, centre yourself, take deep breaths, relax.

Put one or both of your hands on the area of your body that you instinctively feel needs the most healing. Now imagine that there is a pot of liquid golden light in the centre of the room. Breathe into the area that needs healing, pushing your hands out with your breath...

This area in your body is close to one of the seven main chakras, so allow yourself to feel the chakra that also needs healing, and breathe into this area for a moment... Now physically pull it out of you, whatever it is that needs to be released, and make a noise to go with it, as you release it! You don't need to know what it is or why, just do it - get it out of you. Throw 'it' into the pot of golden energy: it is transformed into light.

You have just started your own process of chakra healing!

HOW TO USE THIS BOOK

EXPLANATION OF TERMS USED:

For each chakra I have listed certain qualities that are associated with that chakra and can be used to energize, heal, balance and open that chakra. Below is a brief explanation of each of these, and how to use them.

However much energy you put into the ideas and exercises that are on offer, is as much as you will benefit from them. As with all of life, you will get out of it what you put into it. Also, the spiritual forces will be with you during this time to give you greater assistance!

COLOUR:

Colour is vibration; simply, different rates of vibration give us the different colours. The use of colour will effect your energy field, your chakras, your soul, your senses, you. Obviously, colour in our world is very important; we are magnificently surrounded by it in our natural world. But even the brilliance of a magenta bougainvillea flower pales into insignificance when you can 'see' and experience the 'true' colours on the spirit plane.

Colour is very important to us, it is part of our 'cure'. It is a remedy that our Creator has given us to keep everything in balance. How dreary the world and our lives would be if all around were beige!

Black and white are 'colours' of protection, and are okay to wear … this is the original reason black or white was worn at funerals; as protection against the 'spirits of the dead' at the cemetery. This is also the reason that, traditionally, both nuns and witches wore black.

So let's make good use of colour, our souls need it. **Wearing** the appropriate colour for the chakra that you are personally working on will help tremendously in helping you harmonize that chakra. Having the colour around you in your living and working environment, (flowers of that colour, for example), helps also. Ultimately, it's the vibration of the colour that you need to help you expand your consciousness into the new.

ELEMENT:

Each chakra is associated with a particular element - fire, air, water, earth - so when working on a particular chakra become more aware of that element in and around you, and especially within you. For example, the fire within you, that is, heat, warmth, 'fire in your belly'.

SENSE:

Each chakra is associated with one of the five senses within you. If you want to harmonize a particular chakra, then become more aware of the corresponding sense in you and how well you use it. How you experience each sense may be an indication of which chakra in your system needs strengthening or balancing: for instance, if you have a weakened sense of smell then this could indicate that the first chakra, the Base, needs attention. By developing the first chakra more fully, your sense of smell may become more acute.

SYMBOL:

Associated with each chakra is a symbol, as well as a colour. Meditating on that symbol, with the colour, will immediately bring new energy into that chakra, and movement and transformation begins. You can visualize the symbol over the actual position of the chakra on your body.

LOTUS:

Each chakra is represented by a pattern of lotus petals, and mediating on these lotus petals can help to bring the chakra into harmony.

LOCATION:

The location gives the position of each chakra on the physical body (see diagram 1). This is a simplified guide only - a simple representation of a complex thing.

FUNCTION:

This explains the basic function, or field of influence, of each chakra.

LAW OF CORRESPONDENCE:

The Law of Correspondence is a Universal law, and it operates within the chakras system, as well as many other areas of life. There is a correspondence between certain chakras, that is, there is a relationship between the energies of those particular chakras. By working on one chakra you will also connect to, and work with, its corresponding chakra - you can't work on one without affecting the other. The heart chakra is the only exception to this rule; the heart chakra contains the Divine, and as such stands alone.

As each chakra, except the heart, corresponds to another, the chakra system itself is all connected through the etheric matrix, or etheric 'web'.

GENERAL:

This gives varied and general information about the chakra in question.

KARMIC LESSONS:

Each chakra holds certain karmic lessons or patterns from previous lives within its energy. There maybe certain unresolved wounding from these lives, that manifests as issues relating to that chakra and its corresponding functioning in your physical body, emotional body, mental body and spiritual body. When the soul is strong enough, it will choose to harmonize that karma in a particular lifetime (or lifetimes) and then there will be strong emphasis on that chakra and its issues, to enable it to be healed. Working *consciously* with the karmic issue will release this chakra like nothing else can!

Because these energetic patterns, or even distortions, are so important to the evolution of your chakras, I have emphasized the understanding of karma in general, and the underlying karmic pattern or lesson in particular, as it relates to each of the seven main chakras.

HELP! SECTION - HOMEWORK:

In this section for each chakra, I have given a list of simple, appropriate, tools and exercises that help to change permanently the underlying pattern that may be harming or causing wounding to the energy of that chakra. Although these tools seem very easy - and they are - don't underestimate the profound effect they can have to increase your wellbeing.

It is strongly suggested that you concentrate on only *one chakra per month*, starting with the Base Chakra (1st) and continuing up the body in sequence. You can choose any or all of the tools to help heal the chakra, but it advisable to try at least ten of the tools offered. It is highly recommended that you bring the COLOUR (that is, the vibration) of that chakra fully into your life for that month, especially by *wearing* the colour. So, for instance, if you are working on the Base Chakra whose colour is a true red, then use that colour as much as possible in your clothes, underwear, nightwear, shoes (if possible), environment: that month for you is the Red Month. When you move on to the next, Sacral, Chakra the next month becomes the Orange Month, and so on.

I know it sounds mad, but it works!

I have facilitated the Chakra Course that I developed for very many years, and I (and the students) have seen and felt the changes within themselves, through using these simple methods - particularly wearing the colour. It is interesting to note which colour (s) you have avoided wearing, or have very little of in your wardrobe - have you avoided this colour because it relates to a particular chakra whose issues and challenges you have avoided? This goes beyond simple preference - there is likely to be at least one colour that you find really difficult to wear. The colours that you are comfortable with - do these correspond to the chakras that are well balanced and functioning well in you? Sometimes we become drawn to new colours - is this because we are ready now to work on a chakra and its issues more fully, so we are drawn to its colour?

I give a brief explanation below of how to use each tool suggested:

- **Colour** Wear the colour everyday if possible; if the colour doesn't 'suit' you then try it as underwear, or nightwear, or socks. It is also good to have the colour in your environment for the month, as flowers, candles, paper serviettes, fabric off-cuts, cushions, towels and so on. I realise that it is not so easy for men to be wearing bright colours, but they can still use the colour in socks and jocks, T-shirts, ties and so on.

- **Meditation** The word "meditate" comes from the Latin and means "going into the centre" - and there are many different ways of doing this, not just in a structured way using formal techniques. Musing on a blade of grass or a cloud is meditation - so don't get stuck on the idea there is a right or wrong way to meditate. Please try the different simple meditations given; for instance, unfocusing your eyes and getting lost in the sunset or the blue of the sky. One simple meditation is to visualize yourself sitting in an aura of the colour associated with the chakra you are working on.

- **Breathing** into the chakra area at both the front and back of your body helps to balance the energies - attached is a full meditation on this. You can choose to just concentrate on the chakra of the month breathing; or you may choose to do all of them.

- **Music** is suggested which stimulates each chakra in an appropriate way.

- **Tone/vowel sound** is given to help open each chakra - repeat the tone like a mantra whilst concentrating your awareness in the appropriate chakra area.

- **Stones/gems/crystals** are suggested which help to harmonize each chakra. It is suggested that you wear them on your body, or keep them somewhere in your aura, like under your pillow, in your pocket, or on your desk.

- **Essentials oils** given can be used in your bath, or in a burner or put directly on your skin if this is advisable - check with the manufacturer's instruction.

- **Ascended Masters** are highly evolved beings who have lived on earth in a physical body, as we do now. Through many lifetimes of learning and several levels of initiation, they have ascended into another dimension of existence, where all is pure love. There are many Ascended Masters working closely with humanity now.

  They have great love for us, great compassion, and an understanding of how it is to be in a physical body. Each Master brings a different energy to humanity and the earth, and through this helps us in our own personal evolution.

  There is a Master (or Masters) that is strongly associated with or working through each of the seven main chakras. To help you with a particular chakra, call in the related Master by asking him or her to be with you whilst you are working with that level of consciousness. By using their name and sincerely desiring connection with them, you open the door, so to speak, and they can come into your energy field and into your consciousness much more directly. A good time to call them in, by asking in a firm voice, is just before going to sleep, or again on waking, and of course, when focusing upon a particular chakra.

- **Master oils** are available for each ascended master recommended for each chakra. When applied to the chakra on the physical body, these unique oils will facilitate a more profound and direct connection with the beautiful energies and vibrations of these powerful beings. The Master oils are available through the Cobolt Sunshop online - www.cobolt.com.au

- **General** - there are many other ideas and tools that can be used as suggested for each particular chakra. Don't always choose the easiest ones for you - the most precious lesson is usually in the hardest challenge!

  Good luck!

NOTE

In the text of this book I have for ease of understanding referred to the chakra (s) as being 'open,' when I have used this term 'open chakra' I mean that the chakra is functioning well, it is clear, balanced, in harmony, vibrant, healthy, active and well-developed.

SPIRITUAL PROTECTION

Before we commence looking at each chakra we need to have an understanding of the need for spiritual protection. Spiritual protection is just that - the protection comes from the spirit, or the spiritual realms. It is, in a way, an energetic protection, both a protection of your energies and is given in an energetic form from spirit.

You are protected; it is a natural process. However, when we are consciously doing spiritual work, personal growth or any process where there is transformation or rapid acceleration of the soul learning, we sometimes feel that we need a little extra help.

Here are a few very simple suggestions that may be useful to you if you want extra spiritual protection:

• Visualize, feel or say to yourself, that there is a **brilliant white light** emanating out from within you, extending at least 60cms (36 inches) out from your physical body. Also say *"that this light lets positivity in but keeps negativity out"*.

  (This light is always a divine light, and it needs to be brilliant, like the sun, so that nothing negative can penetrate it).

  Put this light around you each day; say, when you are having a shower, for a week; and then once a week after that if you want to.

• Call upon *Archangel Michael* to protect you, and he and his blue lightning angels will be there instantly.

• In relation to a particular chakra(s) that you may feel that you want to protect, or even close for a while, the following is very useful:

  Visualize, feel or say that there is a **glass cap** over the end of the chakra, do this for the front and back part of the chakra. This will protect and close the chakra. I know it sounds mad, but it works! Try it! This is particularly useful if you are feeling 'too open' or vulnerable, or very sensitive. An example of when you would use this is if you are the sort of person who 'takes on other people's stuff,' usually emotional, like sadness, anger, frustration, especially with family members or close friends. This effects the sacral chakra (2nd).

The glass cap can be removed by you taking it off, or it will naturally dissolve after a week.

At certain times the chakras are naturally more open, they expand (as does your whole aura) - examples of this would be during meditation, and other spiritual work, like yoga, conscious connection to angels, or Ascended Masters, and being in nature. This also happens when we are in love, or in joy. In other environments we will automatically and unconsciously close the chakra(s) for instant protection, an example of this would be when we are in a more astral environment, which would be in city energy, or an office, or nightclub.

All the processes and tools I have suggested in this book are all very normal and natural, many of them are part of everyday life; for instance the use of colour, therefore there is nothing to be concerned about, for your own Higher Self provides all the protection you may need in a general sense.

CHAKRA MEDITATION

CLEARING & BALANCING THE SEVEN MAIN CHAKRAS

This exercise/meditation can be done repeatedly and often, so that you can monitor your own progress!

- Close your eyes, relax: become aware of your breath, take 3 deeper breaths and allow yourself to go into a deeper quieter space.

- **1 - Base Chakra:** Visualize a vortex or cone of spinning energy between your legs, with the tip of the cone pointing to the end of the spine and the wider end of the cone opening towards the earth. As you watch it spin, or feel it spin, see what colour it is - is it red, and if so what shade of red, is it strong in its energy, is it depleted, or muddy in its colour and energy. As you watch it spinning have a sense of breathing through this chakra and breathe *in* RED energy and as you breathe out have a sense of breathing through this chakra again and breathe *out* red. Repeat this breathing process until you clearly see red. Bringing the colour to the same colour red will help clear and balance the chakra. If you can't visualize it, then 'feel' the colour or have a sense of it.

- **2 - Sacral Chakra:** Maintaining the picture of the first chakra move to the second chakra, which is just below the naval. This time visualize two spinning vortices of energy, one coming out from the front of your body and the other spinning out from the back of your spine in the corresponding position. Again, see or feel this chakra, is it strong or weak? Is it moving easily, what colour is it? They should be a brilliant clear orange colour if functioning well - breathe *in* through the front of the chakra seeing orange, and as you breathe *out* have a sense of breathing out through the back of the chakra, again seeing orange. Are the front and back the same shade of orange? Repeat the breathing exercise until the orange is the same strength and vibration both at the front and the back - this indicates that the chakra is re-energized and balanced.

- **3 - Solar Plexus Chakra:** Maintaining the picture of the first and second chakra move to the third chakra in the solar plexus region. Again there is a vortex coming out from the front and another coming out from the back. Breathe *in* sunshine yellow through the front part of the chakra, and breathe *out* through the back part of the chakra, seeing or sensing yellow. Bring them into alignment using your breath.

- **4 - Heart Chakra:** Grass green is the colour of this chakra, and it is situated in the centre of the chest. Repeat the process as described above.

- **5 - Throat Chakra:** The colour for the throat is strong sky blue. Repeat the breathing and balancing process.

- **6 - Third Eye Chakra:** This chakra is situated at the brow area, in the centre of the forehead, and is violet in colour. Repeat the process.

- **7 - Crown Chakra:** This is a spinning cone of energy pouring out of the top of our head, or crown: it is opalescent white in colour. Again, breathe in and out of this area to bring it into balance.

Notice all of the spinning chakras down your body - can you see or feel which ones are strong and vibrant, and which ones are not so clear, or functioning well? The chakra (s) that appears strong and vibrant are open, balanced and functioning well. The chakras that seem to be weaker, or are harder to connect with, are the ones that need more attention.

EARTH CONNECTION MEDITATION

This simple exercise will ground you by connecting you more fully with Earth energies; it will also energize you and at the same time make you feel peaceful. It is very good for the chakra system.

Focus your attention on your Sacral chakra (just below your navel). Put your hand there and breathe into it, pushing your hand out with your in-breath. Feel the area warm up, and then like a laser beam send a beam of light from the Sacral chakra down through your body, through the Base chakra, and straight down - very quickly through the floor, through the earth's crust - down, down through the soil, past the minerals and crystals until it reaches the molten core of the earth.

On the next IN-BREATH draw the energy up from the centre of the earth bringing it into your entire being. On the next OUT-BREATH send your energy down into the earth again like a laser beam - see and feel the beam go down into the earth - and on the next IN-BREATH draw up the energies again into your being, expanding it out through your aura. Repeat this at least five times.

This exercise can be done at any time, anywhere.

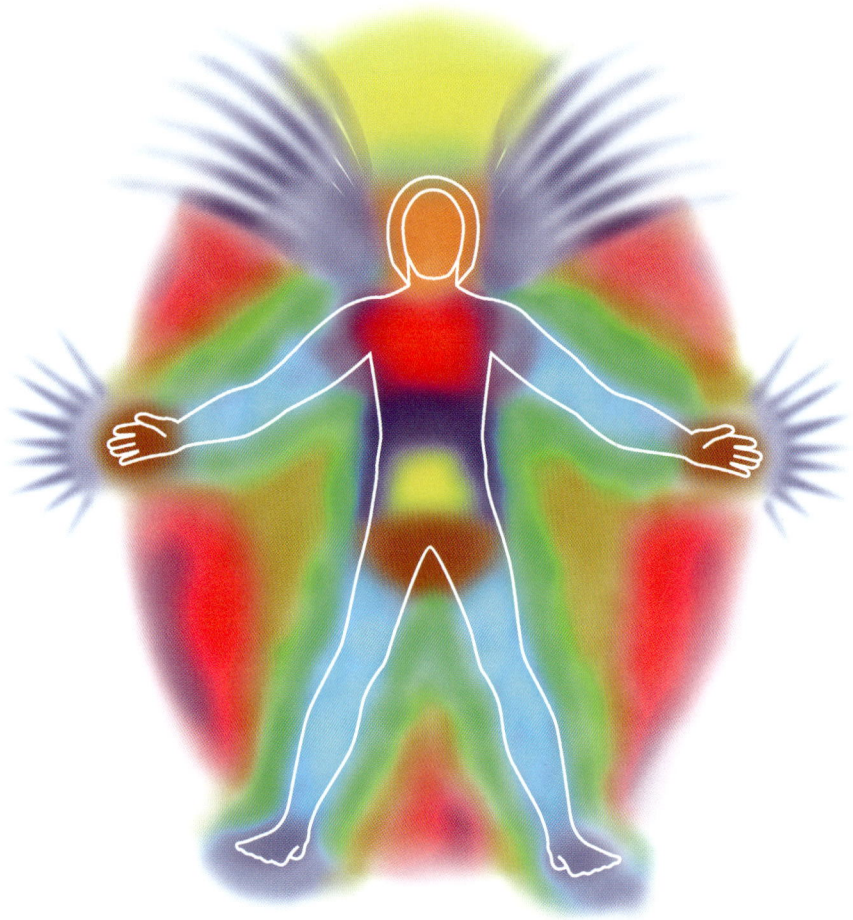

Human Aura

HUMAN AURA

The chakra system is a fundamental part of the human aura; it links the spiritual to the physical, and the physical to the spiritual. The chakras are held within your auric field, and so it is helpful to have an understanding of the human aura.

ELECTRO-MAGNETIC FIELD

The realization of our own power and how to use our energies correctly lies within our greater understanding of the electro-magnetic field. The electro-magnetic fields are more vast than we can imagine, their frequencies so fine, their possibilities endless. We exist in only a small portion of the electro-magnetic spectrum. We are aware of infra-red and ultra-violet light but only under special circumstances; we do not 'see' them normally. This is a hint of the enormity that lies beyond.

This is true also of our own electro-magnetic field (our aura) - it can be so much more. The more we refine the frequencies, the greater the spiritual or metaphysical experiences we will have. The more we realize our own personal power, the finer the frequencies become.

The human aura is an electro-magnetic field emanating from within the physical body, extending out past the physical between 30-40cms (18-24 inches) in an 'average' person. Ideally, it is oval shaped, although many are not. Commonly, the aura has seven layers, though the extraordinary aura (in a highly evolved person - which is rare) has twelve layers, the energies are exquisitely fine and the aura is vast.

These layers are light vibrations emanating out from you. All living things have an aura of some kind - the simpler the life-form, the simpler the aura. Even electrical things, like television and computers, give off an 'aura'.

The Earth also has its own auric field (magnetic field) - with chakras, or energy centres. Different locations on earth have different energies.

This is due to a combination of energies - of living things and events of that particular place. These include the:

• Minerals that are there now, and what went before;

• Plants, now and before;

• Animals, now and before;

• Humans, now and before, and their activities;

• Sun, and other stars, and planets, influence, now and before.

Eventually we will have maps of energy fields here and on other planets, so that we can choose to live accordingly, with our own energy field. We do that now through intuition: "I would rather live by the sea" or "I like the mountains" and so on.

For all living things, the aura that shines out is an expression of the condition of that thing. For us, it's an expression of us at any given moment. Our auras are quite complex, and are made up of basic soul colours that rarely change, and at the same time flashes of colour that depict a passing emotion or momentary feeling. A bright red colour may flash through the aura, denoting anger leaping out towards a person or situation; rose pink shows that the person is in a peaceful, divine, often loving state; blue may show they are wanting space, or feeling aloof; a slimy orange colour indicates that they are telling a lie; if slimy green - then jealousy; a yucky yellow indicates cowardice; colours depicting injury or illness are dark red.

The soul colours are just that - they are an expression of you and your soul's journey so far. You have brought the auric colours into incarnation with you - you have earned them from previous lives.

Your aura is unique to you, yet of course there are similarities between auras. When we look at the aura we need to note where the particular colour is in the aura; the way the energies flow; the vibration level; the shade and amount of the colour - because these things all determine what the colours depict. Because the colours have been earned from past lives, then our past lives can be 'read' through viewing the aura. Sometimes a colour dominates the aura, and doesn't allow the qualities and energies of the other colours to be expressed.

For instance, if the first colour in the aura is a light red, it means the soul is playful, happy and warm, but if there is an over-abundance of blue in the aura (from too many spiritual lives) it will dominate the light red and the person will feel frustrated because he or she cannot express his or her playful, warm side.

The substance the human aura is made up of is etheric energy, astral energy, and spiritual energy - for simplification, we call this the etheric body, the astral body, and the spiritual body. These are all 'light bodies'.

FOUR BODIES THAT MAKE UP THE HUMAN BEING, INCLUDING THE AURA:

Physical body

Our physical body developed as a vehicle of expression for our soul and spirit. It is the temple and as such should be revered and cared for. The physical body is created by four different forces each time you incarnate: your soul, the nature Spirits, the mother's energies and the spiritual forces (God). The physical body should work automatically, as we have spent eons of time developing it to such an extent that we do not have to be consciously controlling our breathing, our circulation or digestion and so on. This is to free us to put our focus into the next level of our learning.

The physical body has the slowest vibration of your whole being.

Etheric Body

The etheric body is the highest or finest form of the physical; although a light body, it can be seen quite easily. The etheric body is the life force (chi) - everything that is alive has an etheric body. So minerals, stones, do not have an etheric body, but plants, animals and humans do. Anything that has a life-force flowing through it has an etheric body.

Etheric energy also provides the template upon which the flesh is built, so we have etheric organs, etheric arms - this is why if we lose a limb we may still feel it there, because the etheric *template* of the arm is still there. One day we will be able to regrow the missing arm or leg, upon the template.

Generally, the etheric body extends beyond the physical body and into the aura only a few centimetres, except around the head where it is larger. In the ancient days, our etheric bodies were much larger and softer. The etheric used to extend around our heads like a horse's head. This meant that the ancient people were much more clairvoyant, and were able to receive impressions, images and 'knowing' through their larger, soft and impressionable etheric energies.

To develop thinking and our own sense of self, our 'I', the etheric body was drawn in, into the physical, and our clairvoyant abilities were reduced.

The etheric energies are also contained in the blood, and as such flow through our bodies constantly renewing us, especially when we are asleep. The etheric body is also the memory body, and the softer and larger it is, the easier it is to retain the memories.

All of nature gives off etheric energy, the most etheric force being water. We know when we walk in nature, or by the sea, we feel calm, relaxed, nourished and full. This is because the etheric energies of nature, especially the sea, nourish our own etheric body, allowing it to expand, relax and renew.

Fire also gives off etheric energy, and this is why we use flowers, candles and incense in our churches and temples, to 'feed' the etheric energy of the congregation, so that they are more able to receive the teachings, visions, and understandings of the spirit.

Healing was always done on the etheric body - often we have had a disturbance in the etheric body for years before it manifests as an illness in the physical body. In the ancient days healers were clairvoyant, and they could 'see' the pattern of illness growing in the etheric, or see the energy stagnating in a particular area, and they could take measures to correct that before it manifested as illness within the physical body. This knowledge will be 'remembered' and used again, for all true healing must reach the etheric level.

Any live performance, if it's good, also gives off an etheric energy that nourishes the audience through their chakras - we get a shiver up our spine as the energy of the chakra is awoken and thrilled by the good performance of any live music, live theatre, live art.

The etheric force is also contained within the food we eat, otherwise it is of little benefit. Obviously, there is no etheric energy left in a packet of biscuits. The etheric is still alive in fresh produce, but when it starts to rot, the etheric energy is depleted. Microwaves kill the etheric force in food.

From this time, and over the years to come, the etheric body and the chakras will be replenished by the spiritual forces, by new waves of divine light hitting our galaxy. This will make the chakras and the etheric body softer, more flexible and malleable, and they will rapidly expand - so your etheric body will become stronger and larger, as will all etheric substance, whether it is the etheric body of a plant, animal or the ethereal worlds.

You will be purified; the more work you have done in the past to dissolve the emotional dross, and leave behind your more rigid ways, the more your chakras and etheric body will respond.

There are tremendous electrical and magnetic energies pouring through our bodies at this time, and the more sensitive you are, the more you will be aware of them. This is all good, but it is exhausting!

Our Earth and our etheric fields are opening to receive more spiritual light, particularly at the time of solar and lunar eclipses.

With all this psychic energy around, we need to be aware of protecting ourselves, because any new reality makes us more vulnerable to 'attack' and raw energies. The etheric body receives imprints, like plasticine does, mainly through the astral - as visions, dreams, 'seeing', and so on - and the larger, softer and stronger it is, the more you can 'receive'. Be a receiver! We will all be more receptive to other people's psychic energy. This can be good and not so good!

We need to support and enrich the etheric body, by walking in nature, by the sea, at sunset, or with candles, flowers, gardening, live art, theatre, music. Trust the process - it is just beginning, and it is what you have been asking for...the beginning can be tricky as you change gears, adjust realities.

This development will help all of humanity to experience and embrace the bigger picture, and to become less petty, self involved, and more genuine, with nowhere to hide, and not so many secrets!

Astral Body

Astral means 'light', or 'of the stars'. This is our star body. It is the body we are still developing, and the one we have most trouble with!

The astral body gives us the colours we see in the aura - these colours and energies are all interpenetrating and in constant movement.

The two basic functions of the astral body are to give us consciousness and to enable movement. Animals have an astral body, plants do not. The astral body gives the animal a limited consciousness and the ability to move independently, at will.

The astral body has many other functions also; it is the desire body, the emotional body and the mental body.

The soul is contained within the astral body. When we go to sleep (or lose consciousness in any way) our astral body, along with the soul, separate from the physical and etheric bodies. That's why we 'lose consciousness', since the astral gives us the ability to be conscious. The reason we need to sleep is that the astral energy wears down the physical and the etheric, so by the astral lifting out during sleep, the etheric (life force) is able to replenish itself and the physical body. When this process is complete, the astral and the soul move back into the physical and etheric - we call this waking up - and we feel refreshed.

The astral energy wears down the person during consciousness because astral energy is like 'city energy' or nightclub energy: it is very busy and buzzy, and stimulating, whereas etheric energy is like nature, or the waves - very flowing and peaceful and relaxing. This is also why, when we are unwell, our natural inclination is to go to sleep, to bring on healing - we let the astral move out slightly so that the etheric and physical can rest from the busy astral energy, and heal. As mentioned above, the etheric is the true healing body, and it works remarkably when the astral body is not 'obstructing' it so to speak.

The astral body, with the soul, can leave the physical body either by lifting out of the front of the body, or via the back of the head (medulla oblongata) or through the soles of the feet. The astral is attached to the physical at all times by an astral link called the **silver cord**. It is through this cord that the astral and soul can instantly return to the body; if the cord is broken then the astral and soul can no longer inhabit the physical body, and we call that death. For up to three days after 'death' the etheric body is still connected to the physical body, this is why the nails and hair (the most etheric part of the physical body) continue to grow. Candles (fire) and flowers are traditionally used when a person has passed on. The original reason for this was that these things give off etheric energy which assists the etheric body of the deceased person to lift, and that helps the soul to move on quickly.

The astral body prepares the physical body and the person for death, by, over a period of time, loosening. This means that the astral body is not so attached to, or anchored in, the physical. Through old age or sickness, the astral will loosen, so that even when the person is awake (conscious) and the astral body is there, they seem only half there. They appear vague, eventually drifting in and out of consciousness, until the process is complete. Sometimes, this can happen slowly over a number of years, as with aging; sometimes it is quickened by the soul through an illness.

If a person is not prepared for death in this way, but dies suddenly and unexpectedly, for instance, in a car accident or act of war, then it can be very confusing to the soul as they hover over their physical body not realizing they can no longer inhabit it. This is when our prayers and loving thoughts are especially needed so that the soul may realize what has happened and turn to the Light, so that the soul does not get stuck in-between worlds.

Where do the astral body and soul go when they lift out of the physical realm?

When the astral lifts out, it can move just a few centimetres, or go to the corner of the room, or it can go much further, filling the Universe. Where our soul goes depends upon several factors - our general development, the condition of our thoughts and feelings, especially just as we are going to sleep; and our physical health.

There is both an etheric realm and an astral realm, both within and beyond the physical realm. These realms all interpenetrate with the more spiritual realm. In the astral realm, or astral worlds, there are seven main levels, from the lowest astral energy to the highest vibration of astral energy. At the lowest are the most dark energies and entities, and at the highest are the most beautiful celestial beings (angels).

Depending upon our soul vibration, which is a product of our soul's learning and progress, we usually go to the astral level that vibrates in common with our soul. Each of the seven levels or dimensions of the astral worlds has seven sub-levels - so when we go to sleep our astral body and soul will generally go to our level of vibration; say Level 4, sub-level 6, so to speak. It is at our level that we will feel most at home, and it is here that our soul friends from this life and other lives generally reside.

If we go to sleep feeling angry, or some other strong emotion, or have negative thoughts, then this emotional vibration will take you to a lower level of the astral than you are normally attuned to - of course, you then wake feeling worse, feeling as if you have been battling all night. This is why we were taught to pray before we go to sleep, and as it says in the Bible (Ephesians 4:26) taught "not to let the sun go down upon our anger." It is helpful to think and feel lofty thoughts or send love to others before sleeping so that your vibration will be of a finer, higher substance which will, like a magnet, take you to a higher level of the astral, where beautiful beings and experiences are. After this experience in the astral, we wake feeling amazing, as if we have been somewhere very special - we may also find it difficult to 'come back' into our physical body.

Alcohol loosens the astral body. We can see the effects of this the more a person drinks; they lose co-ordination (controlled movement) of their body and become less and less conscious. If they drink enough alcohol, the astral leaves totally and they become unconscious (remember, the astral body brings consciousness and the ability to move). Alcohol also reveals that which resides within the person's astral body, for he or she can no longer hide it - and this is also the desire body, so alcohol reveals the desires and lusts. Alcohol was introduced into evolution by Noah's son (after the Flood - at the Fall of Atlantis) to loosen the astral body of the people. The astral body had become too concretized, too rigid and hard. Because the astral is now less fixed in people, we will eventually no longer need alcohol and it will pass from common use and favour, as other things have in the past.

On a personal level, our aim is to open and harmonize our chakras and to purify our astral bodies so that they may be a more suitable vehicle for the divine. The angels work on us through our astral bodies;

as do the negative dark forces. So the astral needs to be of a finer, higher vibration for us not to be seduced and trapped by the negative forces, but to allow the divine forces to be with us more. In any spiritual tradition that you enter into, the first teaching is spiritual discipline. This discipline is to purify the astral body, to give mastery of our lower self.

Spiritual rituals and practices also uplift and purify the chakras, the etheric and astral bodies and the soul.

In a way the astral body is our battleground; we need to be vigilant, because the lower astral energies will pull us down into inertia, into lustfulness, into crime, negativity, addictions and so on. This is the tension within us pulling us from the lower to the higher. The more mastery we have over our lower levels the more pure the astral body becomes, for we literally 'add light' to our astral body, becoming more en-lightened. Life becomes easier when the astral gives off more light - the whole aura shines. The opposite is true of someone who is stuck in the lower astral thoughts, and the aura, because of the astral component, gives off an ugliness, like a bad smell, or a feeling like they need to wash. We may shun such a person, because on a soul level we know that their astral body is 'dirty', and that we may become easily contaminated.

The substance of our astral bodies is easily exchanged between people; this is often desirable, as with teacher and student relationships, or between friends or couples; or parent and child. But it is very undesirable between people whose vibrations are not in sync with one another, where one may 'pull down' or corrupt the other. Even for people who are in relationship with one another, it is important to maintain some astral identity of their own - when a couple has been married for a very long time they can often exchange astral bodies to such an extent that they each have half of the other's - this means they will come to physically look alike, and speak in the same way, using the same expressions. It is particularly through the sexual encounter that we exchange astral energies, which helps us to form a soul bond, but makes it difficult to separate after a time, as it takes some seven years to get someone completely out of your astral body if you have had sex with them.

As with everything, we need a balance of both the astral and the etheric within us. We can be too etheric (dreamy, vague, off-with-the-fairies) or too astral (hard, brittle energy, superficial, glamour-seeking, negative, lustful) and we must balance the two - support the etheric by bringing nature, flowers, plants into the astral area, by having a plant or crystal next to the computer. We become more astral by being grounded: eating red meat makes you more astral.

It is interesting to note that though we die, we keep the same astral body and the same etheric body in a closet, so to speak, awaiting our soul's return for the next incarnation. The chakras, astral and etheric components of the aura, will have the same unresolved issues, and perhaps illnesses, within them as when you last left the physical. They have been dry cleaned, but they are just the same!

Spiritual Body

The spiritual body or soul body is not so much a body as we understand it but more an energy that permeates the human being, especially the aura.

One thing that sets us apart from the animals is our spiritual body, which gives us the ability to develop individuality, our own uniqueness, our IAMNESS. We have a unique soul: each individual has a soul of its own, whereas animals are an expression of the group soul that they belong to - my dog is an expression of the dog soul. Animals also evolve, and may eventually become individuals - we all know of a cat or a dog that is unique or remarkable, and we know of others that are 'just cats', or 'just dogs'.

Your IAMNESS is your divine individuality, the unique being that you are. *The most spiritual thing you can do, is to be the most You that you can be.* Daring to be you, to be true to your inner self, is a spiritual act. When you arrive on earth you try to fit in, try to join the group consciousness so that you will be accepted, loved, liked - that's okay, you have to join the group before you can leave it. But there comes a time when you will feel more and more compelled from within to stand alone, to take risks, and to become your Self, at the risk of leaving the 'group', and even if others don't like it.

KARMA, REINCARNATION
AND THE SOUL

Before we look at each chakra we need to understand the Law of Reincarnation and the Law of Karma (also known as the Law of Cause and Effect), because our karmic patterns underpin and affect the energetic processes of each of the seven main chakras.

Reincarnation means 're-entry into flesh'. The essence of your being, your essential self, never dies. After each incarnation, it is reborn into another physical body, to experience another life on earth.

Reincarnation occurs when your soul incarnates into a new body, inhabits a new vehicle. This physical vehicle, and the life situation surrounding it, have been designed and chosen especially for the higher purpose, learning and evolution of your soul. Of course, since we have free will, it is up to us to choose what we do with each opportunity of life: life is a gift.

The spiritual forces, your mother's energies, plus the elemental spirits of Nature and your soul all work together to produce your physical body. We shouldn't really complain about our physical bodies - we had a hand in choosing and creating them!

For quite some time before it incarnates, the soul will sit in the aura of the chosen parents, particularly the mother's. The soul remains there until the physical birth, after which it will slowly adjust to 'taking on the flesh' again. At this time also, the soul's astral and etheric bodies are reconnected to the soul and physical body. (As I mentioned before, the astral and etheric bodies have been held in a 'closet' since the last incarnation awaiting this time - they still contain the wisdom and the challenges from past lives.)

When we first incarnate, our soul takes up to five years to fully accept the physical body - nowadays, this process is usually much faster. The soul moves in and out of the baby's being until it is used to the physical energies again.

Souls that haven't incarnated into the flesh often before, that is, **new souls**, may be slower to accept or understand the physical - they are often clumsy people, who are still learning how to enjoy the physical or even just how to make this strange physical body work! They are usually charming, pure, innocent and naïve people.

Souls that have passed this way many times before, are inclined to adapt quickly and feel 'at home' and able to 'get on with it' - however there is no great prestige in being an **old soul**, for it may just mean that you are a slow learner!

Until a child starts to have its first memory, at around three years old, the soul is still very connected to the spiritual worlds, particularly in the first year of life. The ritual of **baptism** was originally intended to help anchor the soul here more fully. The sacred words that are used, preferably during the first three months of life, are to help to secure the 'stars' in the aura of the child. These star-lights are brought in with the soul as it incarnates. They are held within the astral body - if there is no baptism then they all eventually disappear except for one. The process of baptism or christening still has this anchoring effect on the incoming soul, even though the reason for doing it has been lost or replaced by another purpose.

Before we incarnate, we decide with the help of our spiritual guides what experiences we will need for our further development. We then choose our gender, race, social status, culture, country, identity, tasks, lessons and experiences.

Throughout our journeying on this earth plane we will, eventually, experience everything, or at least, understand it. We tend to have cycles of lifetimes, where we may keep incarnating in a particular family or group, or tribe, until we have gained the wisdom that we need from it before we move on. We also go through cycles of lives where we are learning about all aspects of a particular issue or quality, for example, a power cycle, where we will learn about all aspects of power: personal, inherited, abuse of, right use of, national, political, spiritual power, rulership, sexual power, the power of great beauty, and so on. As we go through this cycle, we are still learning other lessons along the way, but power will be the predominant theme. All things occur in cycles.

In each lifetime, you come into the physical with a blueprint for your life - though nothing is written in stone, there is no absolute fate, otherwise, where is free will? This blueprint is called a birth contract or karmic contract. I prefer the term 'soul contract' because I feel it is more comprehensive. So, deep within yourself, you know what your life's lessons and tasks are this time around - you know what you have contracted to attempt and to achieve.

We attract situations and people into our lives to give us (and usually also give them) the opportunity to achieve what we set out to learn and experience. Life is often said to be a school - which seems a bit tiresome to me! We do learn, but it is much, much more than that. It is an experience, a glorious experience that is boundless in its possibilities.

Having said that, sometimes it takes many lifetimes to learn one lesson. This may be because we don't 'get it', or we can't see what we are doing wrong, or we are in denial, or we take the easy way out ... However, we are very blessed, because the opportunity to learn this lesson will be presented time and time again - throughout as many lifetimes as it takes.

We have within our soul contract many possible futures (this relates to the tenth chakra, see diagram). This is why 'fortune-telling' often doesn't work, because we always have the opportunity to choose 'a different future'. For example, if we need a certain situation with certain people and certain challenges to learn something about, say, the right use of money, then until we have fully learnt it, we will keep walking down that path encountering those challenges until we can learn The Lesson. (Learning each lesson involves learning on three levels of our being.) However, should we suddenly get it, experience an 'aha' moment, and finally learn the lesson and integrate it fully, then we no longer need that particular situation or those people for that learning. We are then free to choose another possible future, another path ... then new people come into our lives, or we change career, or move country, or have a baby and embark on another lesson.

You may have noticed that after you feel that you have learnt a particular lesson, it seems that after a year or so it comes back to haunt you again - to give you a revision class! This is because to integrate lessons fully, so that they become soul wisdom - which stays in your soul forever (whereas information, and book-learning dies with you) - we have to go through the lesson **three** times. This involves our learning it on the physical and etheric level; then on the astral soul consciousness level; then finally on the spiritual or soul level. This is a natural process - you don't have to try to make it happen, it will anyway!

Human souls do not go back to a lower kingdom of existence; a human soul does not reincarnate as an animal or an insect; but we may stultify as human souls, we may get very stuck and not progress at all.

As mentioned previously, animals also evolve, and may eventually become individuals. Animals evolve through being loved by us, and the spiritual forces. We evolve through the angels, masters, light beings, and other humans loving us. *All* things evolve through being loved, including plants, animals, and the earth.

At this time in evolution, it is not uncommon for the time between our incarnations to be as short as fifty years or so. We *can* come back into the flesh almost instantaneously, or there may be a thousand years between our successive lives. We return when it is most appropriate for us, and perhaps also for the world. We need to come back at a particular time, into that certain vibration and certain consciousness that best suit our soul's needs.

As the process of evolution is accelerating, people are coming back more quickly to learn more, to harmonize karma and so release the higher energies of the chakras.

Many highly evolved souls are to be found in menial jobs, positions of service, as cleaners, hospital porters, road workers and the like. They bring the light to those places that need it just by being there, whistling or humming while they work. Sometimes a hospital cleaner or porter may be more helpful and healing to a person in hospital than the doctors are! Often there are younger and unevolved souls working in high government positions; they are learning about leadership and power. There are also highly evolved beings in prominent positions: such as Nelson Mandela, or Princess Diana.

When we understand this, we learn not to judge a person by their appearance - or at all. We do not know them unless we can see into their soul, and if we could, we wouldn't judge them anyway. We should not assume that the hospital cleaner has no great purpose; he or she may be a great soul doing great work quietly.

To the soul and to the spiritual forces (angels and ascended masters) *no identity or task is any better or any worse than any other.* Each is simply what it is. In the spiritual worlds it is of no account whether you are a King or a pauper, a film star or a waitress - it is your soul qualities, and your soul's purpose, that count.

It is also essential to understand that it is not important who you were in other lives: it's who you are *now* that matters. You are the sum total of all your past lives *right now.* It can be very helpful and healing to know some of your past journeying here on earth, especially if it has an impact on your life now. It gives you a bigger picture, it can make sense of *now*, it can quicken your progress because you may be able to see your lessons, purpose and path ahead more clearly. Sometimes, just realising why you are in a certain situation, from a karmic point of view, helps you release it. The chakra in which the karmic pattern is held is released, and can 'flower'. (That's how it looks clairvoyantly, the realisation releases the energy blocked in the chakra and it starts to unfurl like a beautiful rose, and you blossom!)

Do you feel as if you've had experiences of lives that you lived previously? Do you feel some non-rational connection to other people and places, times and events? These experiences can often come to us through dreams, 'déja-vu', connections with other people, or a feeling that you have known them before, a "where do I know you from?" You may have flashes of images of other places, times, faces. When that happens, it will be relevant or connected to something that is happening now in your life - otherwise why would it happen? There would be no point in your Higher Self making that information available to your consciousness if it had no relevance to your current situation. In the ancient days, when we were all clairvoyant, we remembered our past lives, just as we remember bits of our childhood now. As we develop, we will again become more and more clairvoyant (clear-seeing) and remember our past lives. For this to happen, we need to have our third eye chakra open and balanced to quite an extent, and this then enables the ninth chakra (see diagram) to activate, and we start to 'see' or feel or otherwise know our past lives. Indeed, this is already happening to those individuals who are ready for it.

KARMA

Karma is a quality of time. You cannot have karma without reincarnation.

We have given Karma a *bad* name! The concept of karma that most people hold is that it means that you are paying for or making up for past mistakes from other lives, that in some way you are being punished by God for being naughty in a previous life. Karma is not punishment. *You **do not** begin your journey by being punished by God for poor performance.* God is love.

Karma is a natural law. It just happens - God doesn't do it to you. It is not retribution, or pay-back, and really there is no such thing as *bad* karma - *all karma is good*. It doesn't always feel good when you are going through it, but when you have learnt a karmic lesson, you then bring balance and harmony to your chakras and to your soul, and you feel alive, vital, joyful, free and more at peace.

Karma is the Law of Cause and Effect. **Every action generates a force of energy that returns to us in kind.** We have all heard sayings such as: "what you sow you will reap"; "paying till the last penny"; "what goes around comes around". These are all expressions of the Law of Karma. Indeed, we do pay to the last penny. For instance, if you take a pen from your workplace (intentionally), then you will lose something of equal value.

When the soul is strong enough, we will choose to walk through each life lesson again, to learn what we did not or could not learn before. God is very good to us - we are given endless opportunities to learn, and to harmonize our karma, and so heal our chakras. We do not deal with karmic lessons sequentially; we deal with each when we are spiritually strong enough to go through the circumstances again, thereby learning the lesson (hopefully!).

We may carry something in our soul memory for thousands of years before we, and surrounding circumstances, are ready to deal with it, or we may deal with it tomorrow. The more evolved souls are, the quicker they harmonize their karma, so they can do it straight away. We call this 'instant karma'.

During each of our journeys on earth (and karma can only be harmonized in the physical body, here on earth), we are not only living this life, but are also working on issues that we have brought with us from other lives.

Before we reincarnate, we seek out the situation that we need, so that we can go into it again and *do it differently*. There may be something we refused to learn, or we may be 'stuck' in the issue, or it may be that we need to reclaim our power from a certain individual or group that had taken it away from us in the past (or to whom we had surrendered it). If we have caused pain to others in past lives (with intent, or malice, or by carelessness), then the way we harmonize this is to live a life (or lives) in which we *experience the pain we caused to others.*

The Law of Karma and the way it is all worked out for every single soul is very complex. Because of this, it is organized by very lofty beings, and guided by the Karmic Board. **The Karmic Board** is a reality in the spiritual worlds, where many Ascended Masters and other Light Beings officiate in different capacities. At present, and for some time to come, the Head of the Karmic Board is Lord Sananda, whom we know as Master Jesus. As we know, Jesus came to release humankind from their 'sins' - which, of course, is just another word for our negative karma.

Sometimes a person gets stuck in a groove trying to 'get it' - learn the lesson - and may often have many lifetimes trying to learn the same thing; being presented with the situation again, in order to learn the lesson, the person deals with it in the 'same old' way, often the way they find easiest (such as by keeping the peace, when he or she needs to learn to speak up). They don't try something different, so they continue to repeat the mistakes. Repeatedly ignoring the lesson leads them to experience the situation time and again, but each time it becomes *more difficult*, as the spiritual forces design the lesson to be more obvious, more provoking - they are trying to help the person 'get it'.

We have only spoken about the harder aspects of harmonizing one's karma, but of course there is 'good' karma, where we have created many blessings, and 'good luck' for past deeds that may have been heroic, or caring, or for acts of loving of the unlovable. The good comes when we need it most - a helping hand, an expression of love, abundance, friendship.

The karmic contract is part of the Soul Contract that you have brought with you into each lifetime. With the Lords of Karma, you have outlined in this karmic contract those things which you will endeavour to harmonize, learn and achieve in this life. When you feel most *angry** or most *depressed**, is when you are not meeting the terms of your contract, because at those times you are violating the sacred agreement that you made with *yourself*. Intuitively, you know the lessons, or tasks, before you. If you are angry, depressed or confused, for no apparent reason, ask yourself this question:

'IN WHAT WAY AM I NOT FULFILLING MY SOUL CONTRACT?'

Lessons are recognizable because they are challenging, and feel hard to do - if something is easy to do then it is not a lesson or karmic for you. A good way to see the process operating in your life, is to notice when it is that someone pays you a compliment, pats you on the back, and for a moment it feels nice, but you don't really absorb it - it isn't really valuable to you. On the other hand, if you get excited and *pat yourself on the back* about something you have just achieved, then you know that this is a lesson you have learnt, or are still learning, and it may be a karmic matter for you. When *someone else* pats you on the back, it usually means they are acknowledging a skill, or an ability that you have learnt in other lives, and which is part of you now.

Not every lesson is karmic - some are just lessons that we haven't had the opportunity to learn and experience yet. Sometimes, the struggles we go through are not karmic but are needed for us to refine our gifts, and to make us more conscious.

Some of our lives are easier than others. If we have had a particularly challenging life, then we will reincarnate with little karma so that the life is like a **spiritual holiday.** This is necessary sometimes, so that the soul does not see or feel that life on earth is nothing but suffering, pain and sacrifice. Life on Earth is also joyful, fulfilling, amazing and mysterious.

Nations also have karma, bodies of people have karma, races,

* This does not refer to clinical depression or other medical conditions

groups, families as well as individuals, have karma. We choose where and with whom we want to incarnate according to our desire to harmonize the karma of such groups, as well as our personal karma. For example, people who were or are Jewish will have a certain karma; people who are aborigines or in tribal groups would have a different karma, and so on. Sometimes a great soul incarnates willingly into a family to stop particular family karma or conditioning from continuing indefinitely, which can happen when a particular (negative) pattern is very strong and has been fostered over many generations; they do this by being themselves, by daring to be different from the rest of the family, to show the family that there is a different way of being or thinking. They are born to break the family curse. The members of the family may or may not 'get it' - that is not the responsibility of the different one (the 'black sheep'), all they came in to do was to *give them an opportunity* to do it differently. To incarnate into a family where most, if not all, members do not understand you or value you is very difficult and it takes a soul with tremendous spiritual maturity and strength to agree to it. This person is helping to release the blocked energies in the lower three chakras of all the individuals in the family, and they themselves will have free-flowing and refined chakras through their previous learning and development, which permits this work to be done - this alone can facilitate the healing and release of chakras in other individuals. If you are around someone whose chakras are well developed and clear then this has a positive effect upon your own chakras.

When the soul reaches a certain level of development, it is more sensitive and has more spiritual force and maturity. Sometimes the soul chooses to go into *rapid* mode. It calls down *all* of its karma, to be dealt with in one life, because it is spiritually strong enough to handle it. This usually happens in a life at the end of a cycle of lives, and is an *initiatory life*. It can be very challenging - trouble seems to come down on this soul from everywhere and constantly. But it sets the soul free.

The more developed our soul is, the more we tend to *volunteer* (or get volunteered!) for difficult tasks here on earth. We put our hands up when we are in spirit because we forget how it is to be in the physical: we forget the limitation and frustrations of the physical existence and physical body! We should be grateful to such gung-ho souls who have helped humanity progress, often at cost to themselves.

Karmic illness

Some diseases are karmic, especially those that are 'incurable'. Some diseases come into evolution at certain times, to bring something new to the consciousness of humankind. When humanity has learnt all it can from this disease, we find a 'cure' for it, and it no longer besets us.

Sometimes, our ailments are reminders of past life issues or challenges. Our necks might get a certain pain in it every time we are dishonest or thinking of being dishonest, because in a past life we have been hung by the neck for being dishonest (for theft, perhaps). A person may be deaf, or partially deaf because in a previous life they 'turned a deaf ear' to those that should have been heard. These two examples show how wounding or dysfunction in the Throat Chakra might be carried into lifetimes repeatedly, until the issues that caused the wounding or dysfunction in the first place are balanced, healed and resolved.

Of course, there are *many other* reasons for being deaf or having neck pain, or for any illnesses or issues. We must not judge why someone has a certain challenge - what is right for one is not right for another. We judge from our own limitations. For example, we may see someone who is a surfie, or a beach-bum, spending all his or her time on the beach in the sun, not working or caring about anything else, and judge them harshly - yet living that life may be their karmic lesson; perhaps in a past life they may have been a fanatical priest in the Inquisition and to harmonize that karma and bring balance to their soul that person needs to learn to loosen up, waste time, indulge themself, be aware of their body and enjoy the pleasures of the physical, in a positive sense. On the other hand, it could be sheer laziness and lack of discipline on their part, and not healthy for their soul at all: it is not up to us to judge.

Some examples of illnesses which *may* be karmic:

Cancer Cancer may be a transforming disease, when no other way is possible for that soul to transform. It may also help in the transformation of the loved ones who have to go through it with the person who is ill. The disease of cancer can be held within any chakra, except the crown.

Down's syndrome children

Often this is the last incarnation on earth of these children: they are pure love, and they have incarnated just to draw love out of people. In a way, they teach love. (This is not always true; some may be old Atlantean souls experiencing negative karma.)

Epilepsy   When karmic, this may be due to misuse of one's sexual energies in a past life: if this is true then this karmic pattern blocks the base and sacral chakras.

AIDS   The karmic significance of this is related to bringing sexual activities to a more sacred level.

Migraine   Migraine arising from karma indicates a storing of information that is meant to be shared. This can result in an over-use of the fine energies of the third eye chakra, so that they become distorted.

These are only a few examples of the karmic origins of disease. These are by no means the same for everyone. Each case must be treated as individual.

To harmonize your karma:

- **Repeat lessons.** As mentioned above, you can repeat the process, doing it differently, trying a different approach, moving out of your comfort zone, learning from the experience.

- **Practice.** You can help heal your karma by spiritual practices, such as meditation, yoga, prayer, ritual, anything that purifies and takes you closer to the Divine. All of these will help to open and heal any wounding on the chakra level.

- **Forgive.** Forgiveness relates to the Law of Grace, which is above the Law of Karma - so under grace, karma dissolves. Ask forgiveness from God, and from other souls that you may have hurt, but most of all forgive yourself - it doesn't work if you only pretend to forgive! Forgiveness is not easy, so most people choose the first option of repeated lessons as a way to heal their karma.

- **Appeal.** Make appeal to the Karmic Board for 'leniency', to be relieved of karma. This again is related to the Law of Grace - the nature of Grace is that it just is - there is no way to earn it or get it: it is given by God.
- **Accept Grace.** Sometimes others relieve us of karma, by a gift of Grace.

SOUL

You belong to a certain 'soul stream'. As this is on a soul level, others who are in your soul stream are immediately recognizable to you in some way, and you both will feel a strong soul-bond. Those in your soul stream have journeyed with you for aeons, and have reached a level of understanding, wisdom and consciousness similar to you.

There is love between you, but it is almost more than that ... it is *a knowing* between you, an unspoken connection between you that doesn't need any reasoning, or words. With those in your soul stream, you are capable of having the most extraordinary experiences. In this relationship or friendship, there are different rules, or there may be no rules. Somehow between you there is **freedom in commitment:** a sense of going deeper and deeper.

Those who are 'Beloved' you will always find in your soul stream. These are sometimes called 'soulmates', but I prefer the term 'soul friends', as this is more accurate. You have more than one soul friend, and often they incarnate with you as your children, or friends, parents, co-workers, or as counsellors or lovers.

Of course, we may also experience love, or relationships and friendships with people who are from other soul streams, and although there can be great love there, it is somehow not quite the same. Often our relating with others from different soul streams happens in order to harmonize some past karmic lesson, but not always. It may be some other experience we need - or some kind of soul 'stretching' that interacting with a person of a different soul stream energy can provided.

Soul love is like no other. This 'great love' is unbounded, fulfilling, yet often there is a feeling of not being able to express it fully. It is not necessarily easy living with a soulmate or soulfriend: it maybe okay for short periods of time, but it may feel easier to be 'living alone together'.

Soul love doesn't wound: it embraces, it is creative, inspiring. It can also be very deep and intense - and this intensity may feel too challenging making one or the other run away - maybe they need to wait till the next lifetime!

Soul, spirit and higher self

Your **soul** sits in your astral body, which is part of your aura, and so, strictly speaking, your physical body sits inside your soul. The physical is a vehicle for the soul's purposes and evolution here on earth, whereas the **spirit** is like a force that sweeps through the soul. I see the soul as a vehicle for the spirit's purposes.

The **Higher Self** is just that; it is that part of our selves that cannot descend fully into the physical. We are capable of being more ensoulled, that is, it is possible for more of our Higher Self to embrace the soul and the physical body than it generally does at present. The Higher Self is always in the spiritual dimension, helping and guiding, but it cannot take over the conscious self. The more conscious we are and the more we connect consciously with our Higher Self, the more it is able to express through us, so that our thoughts, feelings and actions are imbued with the energies of our Higher Self. In a way, when this happens, we are purer and more divine.

The Higher Self connects fully to an individual from about the age of four years; and others can appeal to it for help on behalf of a person suffering illness, or other difficulty. When we ascend finally, we fully merge with our Higher Self. In full consciousness we become our Higher Self; there is no separation.

The soul is part of this learning, evolving process, and so is not necessarily pure, or advanced, because it is still learning.

Soul lessons and purpose

Each individual has soul lessons, that is, has things it needs to learn and experience. Sometimes, a person incarnates who has no karma, or lessons, but this is very rare - he or she will have come in order to benefit humanity in some way.

At the same time, and in some lives, (but not every life), a soul may also have a soul mission or purpose. The soul's mission is usually challenging, and is to transform something or bring something new to the world - the *soul's mission* is always for the benefit of humanity, whereas the *soul's lessons* are always for the individual soul's own evolution.

We don't always have a soul mission or purpose, and when we do it is unlikely that it is to be completed in just one lifetime. Generally speaking, it takes about three lifetimes to complete the mission - the first in which you are learning and beginning it, the next where you incarnate and straight away are embarked upon it, and in the last you will be dynamically completing it. The life of Mozart is a wonderful example of this: the soul of Mozart had been a composer in a life previous, but he didn't quite complete expression of it, so when he incarnated as Mozart he was determined to fulfill is soul's mission, and then leave - which he did most powerfully! We are still benefiting from the music he left us. It is interesting to note that the soul of Mozart is again incarnated, and although he is a musician again, he is now more famous for his humanitarian ideals - which Mozart was lacking in. See how beautifully it all works!

The soul's mission and purpose is held within the heart chakra, the throat chakra, and the crown chakra; basically this gives the person the love, will, action and spirit to fulfil it.

Base Chakra Symbol

BASE CHAKRA
I AM

Colour:	**True Red**
Element:	**Earth or Matter**
Sense:	**Smell**
Symbol:	**Square**
Lotus:	**4 petals**
Location:	**Base of spine, spinning down between legs (see diagram)**
Function:	**Survival, physicality, grounding, sex**
Law of Correspondence:	**Crown chakra (7th)**

GENERAL:

The primary function of this chakra is **survival**. This chakra links you to the physical world, to planet Earth. It is your grounding force, connecting you to the Mother Earth, the physical realm. The base chakra is very important, for how can we enjoy being here if we are not connected energetically to the source of our physical life? If you are not strongly 'in your body' then you will find it very difficult to enjoy life in the world - as you are not fully *here*.

The energy of the base chakra gives us the Physical Will of Being, and is complementary to the crown chakra, which gives us the Spiritual Will of Being. These two chakras, through the Law of Correspondence, need to work together in harmony. Your 'spiritual will of being' cannot achieve anything if it is not working well with your 'physical will of being'.

If you want to manifest your dream here on Earth, then the first chakra is the most important for this. Your dream or vision or goal cannot manifest in a practical sense if the base chakra is not open and flowing, and connecting you to the earth and her beautiful energies. This chakra channels the earth's energies up to our higher chakras and, at the same time, helps ground our higher spiritual energies into our physical body. The more we ground ourselves, the greater chance we have of manifesting our dreams here in the real world. When you are truly *present, here* in your body, you become a strong dynamic person who can handle the powers of our world; things like money, sex, success, work and so on.

At this time in evolution, we have lost much of our connection to Mother Earth, and we have cut ourselves off from the natural healing source of Mother Earth. This is particularly true of those living a modern Western lifestyle.

How is your connection to Earth's natural cycles? Do you notice the seasons, the moon's phases, the changing sunsets, the weather, the energy in the atmosphere? I want you to connect more consciously with the natural rhythms and cycles, become aware of the energies around you, be aware of the weather and the energy that comes with it. If we can be 'in sync' with the world around us and work with the energy available to us, life becomes so much easier! If we do this, the base chakra is healed and flowing, and we thrive.

Over the past two thousand years, Western culture has neglected the earthy energy of this chakra and often our own physicality. This is because generally speaking, Christianity and other similar traditions have emphasized **spiritual ascension** whilst being somewhat negative about the physical body - in a way, we have been taught down the ages to get away from the physical and its appetites; 'the flesh is weak' we are told. This was done to emphasize the distinction between paganism and Christianity; and yet we are also told in the Bible that we need to honour our body and see it as a temple for the spirit. The new teaching, the New Consciousness, tells us that the spirit needs to **descend into** our bodies; it does not tell us to ignore or deny our body but to embrace it, to honour it, and to prepare it for the integration of the physical and spiritual.

The malfunction of this chakra is caused by our alienation from the **pulse of the earth.** *Do you feel cut off from your erotic nature?* This is part of the pulse of the earth, of the physical realm. We often have too much unhealthy control within us to allow the base chakra to function well, in other words, we are too controlling of ourselves - it is as though we have been castrated, cut off from our natural life force. Of course, we are not conscious of this, until we connect more fully with the Earth's energies; when we feel the difference within us, then we realize how disconnected we have been.

To help change this we need to allow the comforting and healing energy of the earth to flow through our bodies. You can do this just by sitting on the earth and consciously drawing the energy up into your body. The 'Earth connection' meditation achieves this quickly and easily (see page 16).

When we are about one year old and we start to learn to walk, we grow streamers of light from the soles of our feet, (these come from our energy field, or aura). These streamers of light help to connect us more fully with the earth and its energies. For various reasons, some of us don't want to be here on earth, and so we don't grow very long streamers.

Take a moment to look at or feel your streamers coming out of the soles of your feet - how long do they feel? As with a tree we cannot flourish above earth if our foundation, our roots (streamers) are not long and strong. Here is a simple exercise that helps to connect you to the earth; it will ground you, energize you, and at the same time bring you more peace within.

STREAMERS EXERCISE:

Become aware of the soles of your feet on the floor. Feel those streamers of light going into the earth; how long are they? Now grow those streamers - see if you can lengthen them by consciously sending them down, down, down into Mother Earth and feel more connected to the energy of the earth. Consciously send your streamers down through the floor, the earth's surface, and down into the soil, further and further.

This is a good exercise to do repeatedly for a few minutes each week to encourage your streamers to grow stronger and longer. Be aware of your feet on the ground, how you walk, how your feet feel.

Another primary function of the base chakra is the physical functioning of the sexual process. The base chakra shares control of sexual functioning with the second chakra, the sacral chakra. The base chakra governs the physical aspect whereas the sacral chakra is more to do with the emotional, relating, aspect of the sexual encounter.

A big issue held in the base chakra is *trust:* trust that the basic necessities of life will be met for you, that the basics of life are your birthright, that the foundation of your life is strong, secure and clear. We cannot enter into the sexual encounter with love, freedom and joy if we do not have this basic trust.

When this chakra is working well and balanced, then we trust in life, and trust that our basics survival needs will be met.

Do you trust in life, do you trust that all your needs for survival will be satisfied? Do you feel safe and secure in the physical world? Do you trust your body? Do you feel that it is strong, healthy, flexible, dependable?

KARMIC LESSONS: Life on Earth

The karmic lessons that are held within this chakra - or, in other words, the issues in past lives that have wounded this chakra - are to do with one's physical body and issues of survival. We need first and foremost to accept that we have a physical body, and we are living in it here on earth. (This may sound obvious and easy - but it is not always, when previous lives have been traumatic.)

Generally, the karmic lessons affecting this chakra tend to present as physical karma rather than emotional karma, although they cannot be separated totally. Examples of this would be denial or neglect of the physical body in previous lives; failure to honour the needs of the physical body by not caring for it, by not nurturing or nourishing it appropriately; for instance, by ritual denial of the body's needs by excessive fasting, self-mortification and celibacy as a result of religious fanaticism. Also, abuse to the physical body that is on-going and deliberate, such as substance abuse. For this chakra to repair, to heal, would mean that you would have to take great care of your body in this life, learning to appreciate it, nourish it, honour it, love it and so on.

Denial of the sexual aspect of our life, or abuse of it, such as rape, can also injure or close this chakra. Many souls who have lived lives as celibate nuns or monks, for example, will need to counter-balance this by an emphasis on a much more earthy life, with no denial of the sexual or emotional levels - it may take a few lifetimes to achieve the balance! You have all eternity... In my work I have seen very many old nuns and monks (that is, they were nun or monks in previous lives!) come wandering into my consulting room carrying the past with them. They are still vibrating under the vow they took (perhaps more than once) of Poverty, Chastity and Obedience. Other people still (unconsciously) see them with their religious habit on, and so they are invisible to the opposite sex, and often wonder why they don't have a sexual relationship. There are many other ramifications arising from such vows. Religious vows have an impact upon the soul and its energies, especially if the soul is very idealistic. The implication when the vow was taken is that if you break the vow you are somehow not godly, that God will no longer love you, and so you are damned. This of course, is not true; not then and not now. But it is a strong pattern from the past, and it overshadows the present for these people. If you are blocked now, through taking this vow in the past, then the blockage of the free flowing energies will be at the base and sacral chakras. The base will relate to the *chastity*, the sacral to the *poverty*, and the *obedience* (which manifests in this life as 'trying to get it right all the time') will affect all the chakras. If you feel you are stuck in this type of vow, then there is a simple thing you can do that works - in your quiet time, light a candle, sit quietly and when ready say OUT LOUD to yourself in a tone that shows you mean it:

"I AM NOT A NUN (or MONK) NOW"

This will release you from the vow and bring you into the here and now.

With all karmic patterns that you are carrying in your chakras, and that need to be released or changed, you may at first feel resistance rising within you - an inner struggle may ensue, where part of you does not want to give up being a nun, or a healer, or whatever you once were - yet the 21st century part of you *does want to move on* and experience something entirely different!

We cannot get rid of our past lives, neither should we want to, because each one has given us positive things. To be a nun or monk for instance, is a beautiful thing; we experience devotion, serving in a humble way from the heart we learn discipline, particularly of our ego; it can bring many gifts that we can use now. But it is not positive for us if we are stuck there and cannot move on to the life we are meant to be living in fullness now.

Sometimes we get stuck in past lives because they were good, and we were particularly happy then, and don't want to move on. But the soul needs, demands, progress, movement, challenge, excitement, adventure, life! Going against this soul need can create emotional and physical disturbances, which may result in illness.

Other issues from past lives which are likely to affect this chakra are problems of physical survival such poverty, starvation, deprivation and torture. I have seen many overweight, even obese people, who cannot lose weight, or cannot maintain a steady and healthy weight because they have had past lives where they have lived in great poverty, suffering starvation, or have died from starvation calling out for food. So when they incarnate again, this is the most dire need they have to fill, for it is remembered, held in the astral part of this chakra - "I must eat whenever possible, and as much as possible, for I do not know when the next meal will be …". This results in overweight, as the person is not in a starvation situation now. I have seen wonderful results with overweight people who have become overweight in this lifetime (and others, perhaps) because of the deprivation of other lives, by a simple method. First of all, it is *awareness of the reason* that they have this weight difficulty that helps to release them, and also if they keep the pantry and the fridge very well stocked, and are able to go to the pantry and see the food that is there for consumption, and are reminded that it is always there, they will eventually heal the base chakra and the soul from the past karma. You do not have to eat the food to heal starvation karma - the one thing to avoid is to have an empty pantry or fridge, for then panic sets in and huge binge eating will commence. Again, as with other examples, this is not of course the only reason for being overweight, but if it rings a bell or makes sense to you, then it may apply to you. (Wearing bright red helps this chakra move, and because of this, to wear red helps one to lose weight.)

Sometimes, we see a baby struggling with 'being here' in the flesh again. He or she may sleep a lot, and seem vague and elsewhere most of the time. There are many reasons for this. Perhaps it is a very long time since the soul has incarnated, or else the soul is reluctant to be here on earth because its last experience was very traumatic or unrewarding. An example of this could be a child who spent much of its short life in the concentration camps of the Second World War, and now when it reincarnates it will have a justifiable distrust and fear of life on earth, and this will damage the energy of the first chakra, in particular. If a baby seems to be really alert, bright, alive, and curious, then we see a soul who has probably incarnated recently and is very glad to be back here for another adventure. These souls are often in a hurry - and very tiring for their parents!

We all feel like a victim sometimes, this is normal, but if the victim attitude is strong in an individual then they live from that place - they are constantly The Victim, and it almost seems as though they enjoy it.

If this chakra is closed, wounded or dysfunctional the energy of the person will very much that of the victim. The karmic lesson for this chakra is to relinquish the attitude of the 'poor me' victim; who feels that they are constantly suffering because they have 'no choice' - always blaming, with no sense that taking control is possible. Victims are disconnected from their inner core, or their inner core is frozen, so to speak. When they talk, it is as though they are talking to someone else - there is no warmth. They live in a constant state of fear. There is little or no connection between the seventh and the first chakra energies, so they cannot see the truth, and they cannot look within. They are always tense, and are often physically very rigid or hyper-active.

Victims deny, justify, blame - and quit.

They need to realise that they are the boss of their life! They need to take responsibility and make choices, and also allow the body to move freely, gently, easily, exercising outside in nature. Care for, nurture, indulge and love your physical body and this will heal your base chakra and bring you into your life with vigour! Remember that the physical body is not just for work, it is for pleasure also!

Pleasure Exercise:

In the next month, pleasure your body! Indulge it! In as many ways as possible! How are you going to do that? How does your body like to be pleasured?

MANTRA: I AM

To heal and harmonize the underlying karmic pattern of this chakra it is enough to say or chant in the form of a mantra* the words: **I AM**. This sets off a downward spiral of energy, releasing old blocked energies from the past. I know it sounds absurdly simple: 'how can it be that easy?" you ask. Well, healing, truth and life, are all simple when you know how! Nothing has to be complicated to be genuine, useful or effective - life is simple really, only we have made it difficult!

My suggestion is that, with each of the chakras, you try saying the simple mantra associated with the energies of that chakra, and see if you can feel a difference, after about **a month** of saying the mantra regularly. Any release of negative karma, and the flowing of the energies again in that chakra, will manifest in your body as wellbeing, and come into your life as success in whatever area it is related to.

The tone and intention with which you say or chant the mantra is important. An "I AM" statement is always sacred, even if you are saying it unconsciously (so to speak) like 'I am hungry …" "I am an idiot …" but when we say it with consciousness, that is, we are aware and understand what we are saying, and we put our intention into it, it becomes a powerful sacred tool for healing, clearing, harmonizing and raising our consciousness.

Our aim as spiritual human beings is to be able to stand alone in the Universe, in full consciousness, and to say with joy, "I AM", and to know what that really means.

Process: Relax, become aware of the Base Chakra, putting your breath there, so to speak, how does it feel? Be aware of the energy there - if there seems to be no energy there, that is how it is at the moment. Now, see, sense, or feel the colour of your Base Chakra, feel it pulse - after a few minutes say to your Base Chakra: "I AM". Repeat the I AM mantra a few times, and relax.

Now, how does it feel in the area of the Base Chakra, is there any change? any movement, more energy? more harmony? Note any

---

* Mantras are of God, from the Divine, whereas affirmations are manmade, so to speak. The particular mantras given in this book for each of the chakras come directly from the Ascended Masters.

changes between when you began and after the process, but don't spend time analysing it all. Just do it, feel it, keep trying it and you will get results.

You can of course walk around all day saying "I AM" as long as you do it fairly consciously, not automatically and repetitively. Also, if you feel fear coming up that relates to this chakra, (like not feeling safe in the world), then saying "I AM" with conviction will help you transform the fear into groundedness.

The saying of "I AM" can be done either silently to oneself, or you can say it to yourself out loud.

Wearing red and walking through your day saying "I AM", will really blast this base Chakra!!

When the base chakra is open and harmonious you will feel grounded, manifesting all your needs, you will feel secure, trusting completely in the world around you, and able to see the spirit in all things material and physical. And you will enjoy great sex! If this chakra is working well in you then you have probably had many lives on earth which have been a great success, where you have enjoyed life, been grounded and felt safe here.

When it is disharmonious, your thoughts and actions may be overly materialistic, greedy or possessive; there may be sexual issues, and behaviour seeking thrills through drugs, alcohol, sex, and addictions. There may be an inability to let go, thus 'constipation' mentally, physically and emotionally. The desire to maintain control and possession can result in overweight. There may also be a reluctance to do any exercise, and a withdrawal from nature, not enjoying the simple pleasures of the natural world.

In extreme cases a damaged base chakra can manifest as violence, forcing the will on others. Rage, anger and violence can be defence mechanisms that indicate a deep lack of trust, inherited from many previous lives. Behind the rage is always a fear of losing something that provides a feeling of security, well-being, and the basics of survival.

PRACTICAL HELP FOR THE BASE CHAKRA:

Homework: Choose any or all of these simple tools to help open and balance your chakra. In particular, I suggest that you bring the colour forcefully into your life for this month.

- **Wear** as much RED as possible in the next month! Socks and jocks if nothing else! Put it around the house, get red flowers, red candles, wear a red shawl at home, red shoes if possible.

- Imagine sitting in a **red bubble** of energy.

- Do the earth connection **meditation,** outside when possible.

- Feel the **streamers** in your feet and grow them into the earth.

- Honour and **pleasure** the physical body, give yourself permission to enjoy, to be a bit naughty! Have fun, drink a little red wine.

- **Flirt!**

- Contemplate **sunsets**, especially the red ones. Go into the blood red colour of the sky, immerse yourself in it, it can dissolve blockages.

- Listen to **music**, especially with drums, bass, tribal beats; belly dancing kind of music, feet stomping kind of music etc. and dance!

- **Tone:** a low "ooooh" sound; this sets off a downward movement into the earth. Do it with the earth connection meditation and yoga poses, even whilst dancing or vacuuming and cleaning!

- Wear or have around you **gems** of agate, garnet, red coral, ruby, bloodstone, smokey quartz.

- Use **essential oils** of cedarwood for grounding and serenity, plus marjoram and myrrh. **CLOVE BUD OIL** is the best for releasing blockages in the base chakra. Have baths with just 2 or 3 drops of clove oil in it, this will dissolve dammed up past life energy, free you from old restrictive patterns, release emotional past life scarring, blocks etc. It will unleash creativity, passion and energy! It will get rid of the "root of the problem". ***(It is HIGHLY RECOMMENDED that you have at least 7 baths using this oil; use very sparingly. Do not mix with milk, as it then becomes ineffectual for our purposes.)**

- Dance, swim, **exercise** outside in nature, do Tai Chi, garden.

- **Ascended Masters:** Kuthumi and Serapis Bey - **put any of these Master Oils on the base of your spine to have a more profound connection to these Masters and harmonize this chakra.**
- Eat red food and root vegetables! Drink red drinks, red wine.

Sacral Chakra Symbol

SACRAL CHAKRA
I AM AND I FEEL

Colour:	**Bright orange**
Element:	**Water**
Sense:	**Taste**
Symbol:	**Crescent moon**
Lotus:	**6 petals**
Location:	**4cm below navel (see diagram 1)**
Function:	**Relationship to everything outside of oneself: personal relationships, friendships, money, sex. Joy.**
Law of Correspondence:	**Third eye chakra (6th)**

GENERAL:

This, the second chakra, is about relating to *everything* outside of yourself; this includes the ability to connect with other people, the universe, nature, animals, and material things (like money). From this chakra we also get vitality, creativity and imagination (particularly when linked with the third eye chakra).

The major issues that affect the energy of this chakra are relationships, sex, money, abundance, well-being, and a sense of our own boundaries.

This chakra governs **all** bodily fluids - blood, sperm, digestive juices, lymph, and so on. This chakra dissolves and washes away any blockages that hinder the vital flow. Physically, this is expressed through the kidneys and bladder; on a spiritual level this manifests as free flowing healthy emotions which help us to feel constantly renewed. To block and hold on to the emotions is detrimental to the physical body, draining the vitality. Everything that flows in a balanced way is healthy.

Dysfunction in this chakra often starts at puberty, (that is, at the flowering of one's sexuality). If there has not been enough loving touch, caring, affection and tenderness shown to you as a baby, then at puberty you may reject your own sensual, sexual nature. It may also manifest as an urge to hide, to avoid relating to others, remaining closed to others well past adolescence. (This is, of course, common behaviour in adolescence - we generally grow out of it, unless there is damage or wounding to this chakra, usually coming from previous lives.) A damaged sacral chakra can also manifest as a tendency to excessive sexual fantasies and 'kinky' sexual behaviour, and suppressed desires; sex is used as a drug rather than a sacred expression or union, and there maybe great uncertainty, tension and anxiety in regard to the opposite sex.

This chakra more than any other gives us the ability to experience **Joy**. When this chakra is damaged or weak, you no longer see the beauty in life - you don't feel any awe or joy, and you don't experience the miracle of life. At times, we all forget that life is a gift, a miracle, but those whose sacral chakra is wounded rarely ever enjoy or appreciate life.

Also, if this chakra is not working well, you may feel emotionally paralysed, sexually cold, unable to connect to others, and have a general feeling that life is dreary, dull, and not worth the effort. You may feel a disconnection or dissociation of sex and love, making it impossible to experience both together - impossible to experience each as an expression of the other.

Again, as with the base chakra, the big issue here is **trust:** trust of other people. Issues of trust abide in each chakra, each to do with different aspects of life and self. Once the first chakra is functional, and we have learnt to trust that our basic needs will be met, then we need to learn to trust others so that we can then surrender to relating with other people, in particular through the sexual union. This means being able to reveal ourselves to another without feeling as though we will be judged, condemned or ridiculed. You can only learn this type of *trust in* relationship with other people.

Do you trust anyone? Is there one person before whom you can be completely naked emotionally, physically, and even spiritually? While knowing that he or she accepts you, no matter what? If so, your sacral chakra is freeing itself. This does not have to be a sexual relationship, but it does have to be a friendship or relationship with another adult. If you do not have a person in your life like this at the moment, then *ask* the Universe to send you such a person, and also ask that you may recognize him or her when they arrive! Of course, the best way to attract this to yourself is to **be that** for someone else.

KARMIC LESSONS: Joy in Being

Relationship karma touches most of us. Generally speaking, through the wounding of this chakra in previous lives, we have brought into this life some issues of relating to others, and to our world. Our challenge with this chakra is to relate without imposing severe conditions (on ourself or on the other), to flow easily with what is, and to be joyful in the process of living. Yet, this can be achieved.

The underlying pattern we bring that sits in the sacral chakra is: "LIFE'S HARD and there is little joy." A common experience with wounding in this chakra is that the young child feels like it is *standing alone in a vast empty field and there is no one there*, that no one understands, and there is no one to reach out to ... This is an inner experience that the soul has brought with it from other lives, and whether or not the child is surrounded by loving caring people, it may still have this feeling of utter aloneness, or abandonment. I have noticed occasionally that the abandonment or rejection we blame on our parent (s), lovers, or friends is not strictly the truth of the current situation we are in; we are not being abandoned by them, but are experiencing life through the filter of a wounded or dysfunctional sacral chakra. Indeed how do we really live in the Now, and be in the moment, when we are constantly influenced by the filters of our consciousness, our chakra wounding, and past life experiences - our great expectation! Living in the Now is bliss; it is an ancient teaching but one that is nigh impossible to achieve in the Western world for more that a few minutes at a time. If you live in the Now you are in the present, in other words you are in the Presence, you have no worries as you have no past and no future to concern you, you just *are*.

Practising living in the moment, even for a few minutes each day, will help you to heal this chakra.

As you can imagine, there can be much wounding held in the sacral chakra that we may have brought with us from previous lives, to do with relationship issues, and especially in regard to sex, the misuse of one's own or others' sexuality, and denial or abuse of sexuality, especially on the emotional level.*

People who have previous lives as nuns, monks, hermits, priests, priestesses and so on, are likely to have **consciously** closed down both the base (1st) and sacral (2nd) chakras during these lives, and will spend a few subsequent lifetimes learning to reopen them. As a nun or a monk, taking the Vow of Poverty, Chastity and Obedience, and only relating to God, would mean that the devout person would have to control their sexuality, sensuality and emotions totally, effectively cutting the individual off from the lower two chakras. Allowing the energies and joy of these two chakras to flow freely within them again is to bring balance and wholeness to the soul. As I have mentioned, each chakra is as important to your soul's evolution as any other - no one chakra is any more important; all must be working well and connected with each other.

This chakra together with the Throat chakra is very good at creating martyrs, both in a positive sense and a negative sense. In the consciousness of the ancient times it was seen as a great and noble thing to be a religious martyr, indeed sometimes this is still so. However, the new consciousness is not about being a martyr to others, or to your job or career, children or anything else.

Nothing disempowers a person more quickly than feeling that they must give up their dreams for someone else's happiness. Denial of true self is a big spiritual 'no-no'! I am not suggesting that we all become selfish, or egocentric, but what we need to do in order to balance this chakra is to become more self-responsible. Otherwise, feeling like a martyr all the time ultimately leads to anger, bitterness and resentment, and eventually those stuck negative emotions may be

---

* Abortions or illegal abortionists: Abortions do not create karma - unless abortion is used repeatedly as a contraceptive measure by the same person during a particular lifetime; this is irresponsible. From a spiritual point of view, a foetus (at a stage which may be terminated) is a mass of cells, and does not contain the soul as yet.

expressed in your physical body as tumours, ulcers, depression and suchlike. Sometimes there is a deep guilt, a punishing of self, a feeling of deserving suffering that is held in the sacral chakra and that creates the martyr attitude.

If this chakra is not operating well within you, then you may try to 'fix' and 'rescue' everyone else, but never go within and work on yourself; you may also be unable to give to yourself, so you struggle to have enough for yourself, especially of money. Your life may be full of suffering. Your energy may be stuck and everything seems stale, old. It's hard to see how to change, and be positive, and you don't feel joy or happiness. Do not stay in a situation that depletes your energy for the sake of others, trying to keep the peace.

In the old consciousness we were taught to suffer, sacrifice and serve others before ourselves, to deny our true self and deny our sexual nature and sensual pleasure. We've had thousands of years of this! (This is particularly true of women.) We have been taught to feel that we have to *behave* in order to earn a place in heaven. Our culture still validates self-sacrifice, sees it as noble. We must be careful that this self-sacrifice is from pure *intention* or else it is wounding to the sacral chakra: for self-sacrifice often comes from one's ego.

People who've had lots of spiritual lives are used to serving, so it's quite hard for them to *stop* sacrificing themselves. But you *don't* have to serve to earn a place in heaven, you *don't* need to earn God's love - God loves you simply because you exist! Otherwise He is not God. To be healthy, on all levels, Service needs to come from a place of joy.

People who have a dysfunction in the sacral chakra often don't want to change because their suffering is a **way of making them feel special**. To parade your wounds like trophies diminishes your soul. To share a deep experience or pain with another will bring peace to the soul. This is not a competition to see who has suffered the most. ... so we need to let go of the need to suffer and feel pain in order to feel special, and to develop something that makes us feel special, other than suffering.

What makes you feel special? What is unique about you?

Other challenges that are held in this chakra from past lives may involve sex manipulation games; rape; emotional blackmail; the use of sex as power, either 'luring' men or 'taking' women for one's own gratification. The sailor who has a 'girl in every port' and makes promises to all of them will become blocked on the sacral chakra, which will give him some interesting lives in the future as he tries to harmonize his karma and release this chakra's beautiful energy. From a spiritual point of view, any **promise** you make to another and don't fulfil, must be paid in full at some stage during your evolution. Be careful what you promise! (If both parties agree to cancel it, that's okay.) So the sailor will have a lot of marriages to fulfil over a few lifetimes to heal his chakra! Let's hope he doesn't continue making the same mistakes, or eventually he will feel very trapped by women.

Another common example of past life experience that causes wounding on this level is the breaking of the promise when the bride or bridegroom is left at the altar. This is deeply wounding to the person who is jilted; it feels like a knife searing deeply into this chakra, so that it is hardly possible to stand up. Of course, the person who did not fulfil the betrothal (ie. 'promise') will also be wounded here (and in other chakras) but not in the same way. At times life does not seem fair, but remember *'perfect justice rules the world'*: this is an absolute truth, but we sometimes have to wait a very long time (thousands of years) before we see or receive the justice.

Issues of creativity, being fearful of it or having it suppressed, in previous lives will bring malfunction to the energy of this chakra.

Finally, we incur karma that wounds this chakra when we have excessive unresolved emotional pain from relationships; and when there is an issue which is anything to do with the emotional aspect of money and abundance, and the way in which you relate to money. So we can see that there is likely to be quite a lot of karmic pain held in this chakra by most of us!

Unfortunately, suicide is a common wounding to this chakra, for joy is the opposite of suicide.

MANTRA: I AM AND I FEEL

To heal and harmonize the underlying karmic pattern of this chakra it is enough to say or chant the mantra: **I AM AND I FEEL**. This sets off a motion in you that will lead to you feeling joy. It will release old stagnant energies from the chakra.

Again, my suggestion is that with each of the chakras, you try this simple mantra, and see if you can feel a difference; you will need to do this simple exercise for at least **a month** to have lasting results.

Process: Relax, become aware of the Sacral Chakra at the front of your body, putting your breath there, breathing in through the front of the chakra and out through the back part of the chakra (which is in the same position only on the opposite side of the body). How does it feel? Be aware of the energy there - if there seems to be no energy there, that is how it is at the moment.

Now, see, sense, or feel the **colour** of your Sacral Chakra, after a few minutes say to your Sacral Chakra: "I AM AND I FEEL". Repeat the mantra a few times, and relax.

Now how does it feel in the area of the Sacral Chakra, is there any change? any movement, more energy? more harmony? Note any changes between when you began and after the process; again, don't spend time analysing, just do it, feel it, keep trying it, and you will get results.

You can walk around all day saying "I AM AND I FEEL" as long as you do it consciously, not just repetitively. If you feel the fear coming up that relates to this chakra, like fear of intimacy or relating, then saying "I AM AND I FEEL" with conviction will help you change the fear into joy.

Wearing orange and going through your day saying: "I AM AND I FEEL" will really blast this Sacral Chakra! Saying "I AM AND I FEEL JOY" would be even better!

If the past life experiences affecting this chakra have been pleasant for them overall, then this person loves ease, pleasure, sex, and has a great sense of wellbeing. They allow themselves the joy that comes from liking the self and loving life. They have a healthy, balanced appetite for life, and are not over-indulgent. They trust in their body to tell them the truth about what it is that they are really hungry for. They delight in abundance, are content with the way that life has turned out, are prosperous, successful, resourceful, creative; they live life to the full, are fun, happy, enthusiastic, active, and enjoy exercising outdoors.

They always know and trust that there is *enough*. In our culture there is a belief in *scarcity and lack - this brings much wounding to the sacral chakra*. Those with a healthy sacral chakra experience great abundance, because they *know* there is enough to go around.

If this chakra is strong and bright the person has plentiful and harmonious warm relationships, fellowship, likes all things that give pleasure - touch, music, dance, food, sex; has true enjoyment of these things for what they are, and is not trying to impress others with these things, (an act of ego). This person knows the difference between indulgence and abundance, and chooses the latter.

The greatest thing that you can do for the healing of this chakra is to be loudly, excessively, unjustifiably happy and joyful in public! *Do it for the next month!* Practise liking and loving your self. Do things you really enjoy, for no reason other than for joy, pleasure. Eliminate all sacrifice for the next month.

Remember! Orange is for Joy!!

PRACTICAL HELP FOR THE SACRAL CHAKRA

Homework: Choose any or all of these simple tools to help open and balance your chakra. In particular I suggest you bring the colour forcefully into your life for this month.

- **Wear** orange, as much as possible for the next month. Have orange flowers, underwear, candles, cushions etc. Orange stimulates renewing, frees us from rigid emotional energy patterns, frees up the sexuality, increases joy, enables ecstasy. (There are not many models for joy around - we have to be our own model, and create our own joy!)

- **Visualise** orange light, meditate in it, breathe it. _Meditation: Briefly do grounding into the earth through the base chakra, then breathe in and out 'orange' through the sacral chakra; have a sense of being immersed in a brilliant orange light, feel the joy, happiness, and lightness of being._

- _Meditate_ with eyes open on moonlight over water - that will really open up the chakra!

- Listen to fun _music_, carefree, sing-along, happy music.

- **Tone:** low "ohh" as in "November": do it in meditations or while cleaning etc. Say "Oh!!" as often as possible, to get into the spirit of expressing awe, noticing things, surprise. In many languages, "Oh!" expresses astonishment.

- **Gems:** Carnelian, moonstone, citrine, tiger eye, smokey quartz, gold - have them in your aura.

- **Essential Oils: Ylang-ylang** clears dammed up, turbulent emotions so that the feelings can flow. **Sandalwood** increases sexuality, elevates sexual union to the level of a spiritual experience. It connects the 2nd and 6th chakras and gives great opportunities for spiritual experiences through sex.

- Ask for a **miracle** to come in a perfect way. Expect it to happen!

- **Flirt more!**

- **Eliminate all sacrifice** for the next month - leave NONE!

- Eat **orange** food, orange drinks, orange water.

- Ponder on what gives you **joy** and vitality. *(What makes you happy? What gives you joy? What are some things you can do for yourself that YOU enjoy?)* There is no need to impress anyone this month, just do what you enjoy.

- **Exercise** with tai-chi, martial arts, yoga, tantric exercises, moving meditations, walking meditations, cycling, swimming (under moonlight!). Be in the moment; focus on what the body is doing.

- Open yourself to goodness in the moment! If you're not here now, you're never going to experience joy! You must **be in the present** to witness the miracles of life. It's only in the moment *now* that things happen.

- **Ascended masters: Lord Kuthumi, and El Morya.** Ask for them to be present with you this month. **Apply these Master Oils on sacral chakra to have a more profound connection to these Masters and to harmonize this chakra.**

Solar Plexus Chakra Symbol

SOLAR PLEXUS CHAKRA
I AM AND I CAN

Colour:	Sunshine Yellow
Element:	Fire
Sense:	Sight
Symbol:	Circle within which is an inverted equilateral triangle
Lotus:	10 petals
Location:	Centre of waist, just below ribcage (see diagram)
Function:	Your relationship with yourself; it is the Seat of Power
Law of Correspondence:	Throat Chakra (5th)

GENERAL:

This, the third chakra, is a highly complex chakra, being connected to many smaller chakras; but we will treat it as one main chakra.

There are two main functions of this chakra. The first governs how you **relate to yourself**, from which arises genuine self-worth, self-esteem, self confidence and so on (not ego!) and also, **self-doubt**. The other function of this chakra is that it is **the seat of your personal power**.

The solar plexus chakra is our inner light, our inner sun. We absorb the solar energy (the sun's energy) in a concentrated manner through this chakra, which then nourishes our etheric body, which in turn helps to revitalize our physical body. So, for us to feel alive, confident and happy, it is very important that this chakra is working well.

Unfortunately, self-doubt seems to exist in plague proportions. Self-doubt creates a negative energy that works like a toxin in our body that, from a spiritual perspective, makes the blood 'heavier'. On a spiritual level, our blood* carries our life force (our etheric force) and our karma, so too much self-doubt will make our life force weak, our energy low, and life on earth very dreary; it will also make our karmic lessons feel more difficult. We may feel heavy, burdened, hopeless.

The more you doubt yourself, the less empowered you feel; the more genuine self worth you have, the more empowered you are.

Most people have disharmony in this chakra, because of their self-doubt - some healthy self-doubt and introspection may be necessary, so as not to become foolish, but to live from a place of constant self-doubt stops us flourishing.

On many levels, the energy of this chakra digests and transforms our lower energies into higher energy. The solar plexus chakra is connected to the liver on the physical level - the liver transforms substances that we take into our body into either the useful or the useless. It is interesting to note that if our liver is not functioning well, we turn yellow, our skin turns yellow - which is the colour of this chakra!

It is important that this chakra is open and balanced, otherwise we experience digestive problems and, or, issues relating to our nervous system. If we have had a shock, or if we are really stressed, this chakra closes immediately, which may make it difficult to digest food, and we may become 'nervy'.

The general state of our mood depends upon how much light we allow to shine within ourselves - we all feel gloomy sometimes, but there are some people who feel like that all the time. If we feel blocked, miserable, unbalanced, then we tend to project that same feeling onto the world around us, and everything in the world also seems miserable. If this chakra is working well then it will allow much more light to shine within us in a balanced way, and then our world seems brighter. The more clear our solar plexus is, the more we can see the truth of any situation; we can also see more clearly the manipulative behaviour of

---

* **Note**: Once blood is taken out of the physical body of a person, it is just a physical element, and no longer contains the etheric or karma of the person. Should a blood transfusion be required, then it is perfectly safe to use others blood; once it is transfused into the person requiring treatment it is assimilated by their own energy.

others. This is where we get the sense of 'gut feelings'; it is *where* we feel 'gut feelings', and also how we are able feel them.

POWER

If this chakra is balanced and strong in a person then they will be experiencing and expressing a measure of personal power. This may attract others to them who have little or no power, and they may feel that they are being 'invaded' by these less powerful people. These people's projections or invasions penetrate our energy field, and we can feel these disturbances in our third chakra; it is a 'getting' or grasping feeling, as though tentacles are dragging something from you. Sometimes, it may be that they want something physical from you, like money or sex, or it may be your knowledge or love or strength. Instead of approaching us in a conscious, honest, direct way, they unconsciously invade our boundaries trying to get what they want by drawing through our solar plexus chakra.

It is interesting to note that it is through the sacral chakra, the second chakra, where we *take on* others' 'stuff' and the urge to 'do it for them'; that is, we draw in their pain, their anger, sadness, and grief and then express it for them. We must remember that taking this 'stuff' on, taking it from them, does not heal them or help you. Whereas, it is on the level of the solar plexus chakra, the third chakra, that the reverse happens: that is, we feel that others are invading us and drawing *from* our energy field in an inappropriate way.

Envy is the negative aspect of power. **Envy** is wanting what someone else already has that you do not. **Jealousy** is fearing the loss of something that you think you already have to another.

Envy surfaces when we see another person, someone we know or maybe a hero, film star, musician or politician, **who has actualized what is latent within us**, who has manifested what we desire, or our purpose, or gift. What is *envied most*, is what is *desired most*. We all have different desires, wishes, dreams - *why is that*? Because our dreams (our aspirations, not night-time dreams) are our destiny, they are the blueprint for our life - that is why they are there. Within yourself, you want to be that great musician or leader or politician … You cannot envy something in another person if it is not already in you waiting to be manifested. So, envy can be used positively in this sense, to help us identify what we hold within us.

If this chakra is working well, then you accept yourself, and know a love of self that is without ego, giving you an inner peace. You know your place in life, in the Universe; you can look up at the stars and know that you belong. You know you are unique. You are full of light and energy. The light that radiates from this chakra envelops your whole body and aura, and protects you strongly from any negativity that may come toward you.

If the solar plexus is not open or working well, then there is a need to control the inner and outer world in order to feel powerful - this person is not able to access their real inner power because their solar plexus chakra is damaged.

Often this chakra's energy doesn't flow well in those who have felt a lack of acceptance and acknowledgement from those close to them, as a child and adolescent, which makes it difficult to develop a sense of self-worth. So then as adults they tend to seek approval or recognition from other people or through material things; this makes them feel subconsciously inadequate or inferior, and creates self-doubt. Whenever we seek approval from other people we are *giving our power away*, because then at any given moment other people are able to make us happy or sad, so they are in power, and not we. We need to bring that power back to ourselves, give ourselves approval, love, recognition and acceptance, and not seek it outside of ourselves. Of course, as soon as we start to give these things to ourselves, then that which we sought outside of ourselves comes to us immediately and effortlessly from others - because we are no longer grasping for it. This helps us to step into our power.

Wounding on the solar plexus level can result in a person being constantly overwhelmed by emotion, or, on the other hand, finding it difficult to feel or express any emotion.

KARMIC LESSONS: Power

If you have been the victim of a misuse of power, or you have misused your own power in a past life, then there will be stuck past life energy held within the solar plexus chakra, which will distort the chakra. Sometimes, refusing to use your power when called upon will also wound this chakra very deeply - the greatest damage is done to us when we do it ourselves.

Many souls have past life wounding on this level from lives where there has been public humiliation or ridicule, and many have wounding from the time of the Inquisition, when both men and women accused of being witches or heretics were ducked and burned. These, and other people who have been tortured and killed for *just being who they are*, perhaps for being Jewish, or for being a healer, or for being different in some way, experience damage to the solar plexus chakra.

When a person goes through a traumatic experience, particularly if they die as a result, then whatever is in their soul when that person dies is locked away and causes the wounding in the chakra. The wounding pattern that is in this chakra is "IT'S NOT O.K. TO BE ME". When the soul incarnates again this underlying pattern will be active in them, causing malfunction of the solar plexus chakra. They will feel "It's not ok to be me, so who will I be instead?" and cast around looking to see what is acceptable in their world, and become *that*, rather than expressing who they really are. This person has to incarnate again and again as they consciously learn that it *is ok* to be themselves, and that it is *more than ok*.

There is a great sense of betrayal associated with this chakra, especially if this has been our experience in previous lives.

Because of the damage to the solar plexus chakra, the soul may choose many lives on earth in which it tries to hide, to be invisible, or live in seclusion; this is may be helpful for a while, as the soul adjusts again to being here, and learns to trust itself and life on earth; slowly, slowly, it learns it's okay to be and express its true self. But it is not helpful to the progress of the soul if the person keeps on incarnating lifetime after lifetime in 'hiding'. There are many ways to hide in and from our society, and this was particularly true in the past; you could live in retreat as a monk or nun, or a hermit, or be a maid in a large household, or any other type of servant, unnoticed by anyone. Being a civil servant now, for instance, may be a good way to hide - it may also be a good way to serve.

Do you want to be invisible? or does it seem that you are invisible to others? Then it may be that you are protecting yourself, perhaps unconsciously, because of damage to this chakra from previous lives.

What energy are you radiating from your solar plexus? Does it say "Ignore me, I'm not important", or does it say "I'm happy being me, I feel strong, I stand in my power." It is essential to acknowledge yourself, and through this, to empower yourself and move on from being stuck in this self-defeating energy of "I'm not okay."

We must stop the plague of self-doubt that permeates the earth, we need to realize who we really are, and allow ourselves to be that. It is crucial at this time in evolution that we do not let the solar plexus chakra stop us from fulfilling our purpose, both as an individual and collectively. Too much self doubt, lack of self-worth, or self-confidence, and too much humility can stop you from fulfilling your purpose.

If you have been successful strategists, soldiers, leaders, warriors, kings, queens, shamans, politicians, in the past, then this chakra will function harmoniously and you will know your own power, will be self-confident, but without excessive ego. You will be strong, dynamic, and very visible! You can say 'No', stand up for yourself, and take a stand in life. The energy of the solar plexus is quite masculine in nature, being active, positive, aware, energetic.

The solar plexus energy needs to be linked to a balanced third eye chakra (brow) and crown chakra so that there is no *misuse* of power, and so that we do not become puffed up with our own self-importance.

MANTRA: I AM AND I CAN

As with the previous chakras, to heal and harmonize the underlying karmic pattern of this chakra you can use a mantra, and the mantra for the solar plexus chakra is: **I AM AND I CAN**. This sets off a dynamic energy within us, releasing the sense of limitation and betrayal from the past.

Again, my suggestion is that with each of the chakras, you try this simple mantra, and see if you can feel a difference; you will need to do this simple exercise for at least **a month** to have lasting results.

Process: Relax, become aware of the Solar Plexus Chakra at the front of your body, putting your breath there, breathing in through the front of the chakra and out through the back part of the chakra (which is in the same position only at the back of the body). How does it feel? Be aware of the energy there - if there seems to be no energy there, this is how it is at the moment.

Now, see, sense, or feel the **colour** of your Solar Plexus Chakra. After a few minutes say to your Solar Plexus Chakra: "I AM AND I CAN". Repeat the mantra a few times, and relax.

How does it feel in the area of the Solar Plexus Chakra, is there any change? ... any movement, more energy? ... more harmony? Note any changes between when you began and after the process; again, don't spend time analysing, just do it, feel it, keep trying it and you will get results.

You can walk around all day saying "I AM AND I CAN" and you will be the Warrior! You will feel, and be, determined, strong, detached and a leader.

If you feel fear arising that relates to this chakra, like fear of standing in your power or using your power, or you find that in some way you are doubting yourself and lack confidence then say "I AM AND I CAN" with conviction and see how this instantly helps.

Wearing sunny yellow and going through your day saying: "I AM AND I CAN" will really blast this Solar Plexus Chakra!!

PRACTICAL HELP FOR THE SOLAR PLEXUS

Homework: Choose any or all of these simple tools to help open and balance your chakra. In particular I suggest that you bring the colour forcefully into your life for this month.

- **Yellow everything:** particularly clothes, balloons, food, drink, flowers. This helps to strengthen the nerves, thoughts, mental processes, intellect, aids the digestive system, helps to activate and energise. To heal and open this chakra needs the vibration of yellow.

- **Breathe** into the solar plexus. Get out in the sun and breathe the sunlight into the solar plexus. Draw the rays into this chakra and feel them expanding through the aura; it is deeply relaxing to let the sun flow through the entire being, very healing for the etheric body.

- **Meditate** on this chakra, as above, breathing yellow light or sunlight into the chakra, front and back. Visualize sitting in a yellow light.

- **Meditate** on fields of sunflowers, corn or wheat; merge into them with your eyes open.

- Listen to fiery **music** and rhythms-Spanish, Caribbean etc.

- **Tone**: "O" as in "God" (short vowel sound). Repeat to self often, like a mantra.

- **Stones** to wear or have in your aura (in your pocket, under your pillow) are Tiger eye, amber, topaz, citrine.

- **Essential oils** of lavender, bergamot, rosemary. Put these on your body, in baths, in an oil burner. These will help the nervous system especially to relax, and dissolve clouds in the solar plexus.

- Karma **yoga**.

- Say "NO!" but say **'YES to life'**. Be grateful - for 5 things each day.

- Be the **warrior**, not a servant. Be visible, strong, assertive, active, a leader.

- **Do something brave** and courageous this month that you haven't allowed yourself to do before. It can be anything: trying a new sport; ringing a person; a trip alone; study; talking to someone you haven't been able to - these things help strengthen this chakra.

- Tai chi, **exercise**, movement, dance, yoga are all very good for this chakra.

- **Deep massage** of the solar plexus and abdomen.
- Call back any projections of power that you've given away in the past. Choose one person (whoever just entered your head) and do it in love. **Call your power back** to you, even if it was something from years ago that you think is no longer significant...your soul has brought that person into your thoughts for a purpose.
- Let the light you shine on others **shine on yourself**!
- **No self-doubt** for the next month! Let any self-doubt bounce off your brilliant sunny aura. Value yourself. Too much self-doubt and too much humility stops you fulfilling your soul's purpose.
- **Ascended masters: Djwal Khul and Lord Helios.** Ask them to come to you, in meditation, or before sleep - ask to have an experience of them. **Apply either of these Master Oils on solar plexus chakra to have a more profound connection to these Masters and harmonize this chakra.**

The solar plexus chakra needs to be harmonized to some degree before we can move on to the path of love - the heart chakra.

Heart Chakra Symbol

HEART CHAKRA
I AM LOVE

Colour:	**Grass green & rose pink**
Element:	**Air**
Sense:	**Touch**
Symbol:	**Star of David (six-pointed star) within a circle**
Lotus:	**12 petals**
Location:	**Centre of chest, and corresponding place at the back**
Law of Correspondence:	**The heart is central, without particular correspondence**
Function:	**Perfect union through love**

GENERAL

This is the only chakra of the seven main ones that stands alone; in other words, unlike all the other chakras, it has no correspondence with another chakra. This is because this chakra contains the Divine, and nothing can touch the divine. It has, more than any other chakra, the Christ force and the Buddha force working through it.

This chakra relates in our physical body to our thymus gland, our heart, upper back, lungs, blood and circulatory system, and skin.

We understand a lot about the heart, we talk about it often, and when we do we are really talking about our ability to love. When we speak of the heart, or touch our chest, we don't think that this beating muscle that lies within our chest is the thing that loves. It is from the energy of the heart chakra that love pours out both from the front of you and from the back of you. Through this chakra we experience love, joy, community, unity, delight, peace, forgiveness - and many more of these divine qualities.

Touch is very nourishing to the heart chakra, and holding hands is the easiest way to experience the heart chakra. When you are holding hands with someone, the energy goes straight to heart. We also get a sense of being 'in touch with life' through the heart chakra.

The heart centre connects the lower three physical and emotional chakras with the upper three chakras which are mental and spiritual in nature. Here in the heart both the cosmic energies from above and the earth energy from below meet within us - it holds the balance between the physical and non-physical realms. This is depicted very well in the heart chakra symbol with the two triangles which make up the Star, one pointing up and one point down, and the perfect balance of those.

As we know, the heart is the most important organ in the physical body and is known as 'The Emperor' in Chinese medicine. Love is necessary for all levels of existence; many scientific experiments on love and touch have proven what we all knew - that love profoundly affects physical, emotional, mental, and spiritual growth.

Through the heart chakra we empathize and sympathize, as well as perceiving beauty in ourselves and others. Also through this chakra we appreciate Nature and the Arts. Words and sounds are transformed into feelings - giving us music, poetry, visual art, and so on.

In some women the heart chakra can be too open, as if it is going off to one side; this happens when we 'love too much'. It is not strictly true that you can love 'too much', but those who give and give from a heart level, and who do not balance the giving with the receiving of love in return will create an imbalance in the energies of this chakra.

In men it is the heart chakra that tends to need most development, whereas in women it is the throat chakra. This is a generalization of course, for many men have good, loving, open, heart chakras, and some women have open, balanced, throat chakras.

The purpose of the heart chakra is to achieve perfect union through love, and when achieved this brings us to bliss, enlightenment, nirvana. We are all yearning through the heart chakra for deep loving contact, so that we can experience harmony, union, and bliss; not only with other people, but also with Nature, the stars, cosmos, and the spiritual beings that we work with. Sometimes we get a glimpse of this, but very few of us live in a perpetual state of bliss at the moment. But this is our aim.

The lessons of the heart chakra are often learnt through experiencing pain, sorrow, loss, grief, separation, and even the death of others. Often this painful process helps us to achieve the perfect union that we are yearning for.

Unconditional love is what we are aiming for, a form of Divine love. Such love exists only for its own sake, therefore, this love cannot be possessed and neither can it be lost - it just is. When the heart is connected to the higher chakras, the third eye and crown, love transforms itself through the heart into divine love. This then makes us much more aware of the divine in our self, and in others. On our way to this level of loving, our heart has to go through many lessons to learn, to understand and to accept.

One of our greatest challenges at the moment is to love ourselves unconditionally - right now, just as we are, not when we've lost weight, or found the perfect partner, or our perfect purpose, or whatever.

The solar plexus chakra must be functioning quite well in order for the heart chakra to be open. It is as if the solar plexus chakra is a gateway to the heart, and it doesn't have to be completely open, but just working in a balanced way. As we know, the solar plexus is an emotional centre; when clear, bright yellow energy moves through here it travels up to the heart chakra which then gives us the ability to feel what I call the higher feelings, a higher vibration of energy than emotion. Feelings originate directly in the heart; before the solar plexus and heart are harmonious, we experience our emotions rather than our feelings. The emotions originate from the first three chakras. We feel feelings, but are more inclined to be driven by our emotions; generally we are in charge of our feelings, but often our emotions are in charge of us.

Like the base chakra, the heart chakra can be experienced very physically. It is easy to feel the heart opening or closing, particularly if we are going through some crisis or pain generated around heart chakra issues.

When the heart opens more fully, 'boundary' difficulties may be felt, due to the intense feelings that are beginning to flow out. This is because our sense of ourselves, where we begin and end, becomes less firm, and so we become oversensitive or raw to any of the forces that are around us. This happens until we get used to having a more expanded heart, full of love. This can make it hard to be in crowds, or at supermarkets for example, as you feel everything so deeply; you may also feel tremendous compassion, feeling the pain of others piercing your heart. Compassion is the quality that Lord Buddha brings to us, through the heart chakra; it is the highest form of passion. The Christ force brings us Divine love, and is also working very strongly through our heart chakra at the moment.

Feelings are the greatest way to unblock the heart chakra, so it is important that we feel things intensely. Any life experience or therapy or form of the arts that allows that energy to flow through the solar plexus and heart is very healing, and healthy for our consciousness.

A wonderful way to open the heart chakra is to get a dog! This works especially well for children. If we can feel intensely and allow these energies to move through us ("feel it to heal it!") we can spontaneously process childhood or even past life issues locked away in the lower three chakras. Feelings move through very quickly if we let them, but they are not always easy or pleasant. But neither is the alternative, of storing them away in our body.

Tears release the heart chakra and also re-energize it. The extra flowing water in the body keeps the heart cool, and the heart can process the spiritual fire or force within you. So tears are very important - the kind of tears that are releasing, not the tears we cry when we should stay angry instead, that's a different force. Tears produce softness - softness is an open heart chakra.

Bereavement, the death of others, often opens our heart chakra; including the death of relationship, our status or way of life.

Love is the *only real thing*; love is god, god is love. Love is the force that links us all together, soul to soul, cell to cell. If you feel loved you are a different person than you are if you don't feel loved. If you are really loved by someone, with any form of love, you are linked to that soul forever, regardless of whether they have passed on, or you are divorced, have moved on; whether either one is incarnated or not, there is a spiritual link between these souls forever. Whatever lasts in our world, lasts because of love. Anything created in love will persist, whether it is art, poetry, literature, sculpture, architecture, music. The human race persists because of love.

To be love and be loving does not earn you karmic points; there are no brownie points or good karmic points for loving. There are no rewards. Love just is.

Love is the only lesson, to which all other lessons lead. Whether it is a lesson about jealousy, lust, money, or greed, really the lesson is about love. The lessons of love are what love brings up in us - when we dare to love. What does love provoke in us? - these are the lessons.

We often pretend that love doesn't matter to us, but we all know in our hearts that it is the *only* thing that matters, there is no substitute. When someone is dying, we see how love really heals; years of conflict melt away in moments, in the light of love. One day we will love in this unconditional way all the time, but at the moment we are still learning about love.

When we fall in love we are the most alive and joyful we can possibly be! We see everything through the eyes of love, everything is marvellous! This is the realm of love; this is where we have come from originally, and where we are journeying back to.

All true healing is done through the heart chakra, so a good healer must have his or her heart chakra functioning well. Do not separate yourself from that part of you which is causing you pain, whether it be physical or emotional pain; bring it back into the community of your being and embrace it with a loving energy. Separating it out will not heal it, not loving it will not help it - *love it*. Love unifies; 'no love' or negativity separates that which is within and without. It is through love that the greatest potential for the healing and transformation of ourselves and the world is possible.

When the heart chakra is open energy streams out and connects strongly to those we love - streamers of love are exchanged between loved ones, and this can have spontaneous healing effects on others.

The **green** aspect of this chakra is love, healing, harmony and balance. If there is also a **rose** pink colour present in the heart chakra it identifies a person who lives in pure and selfless love of the Divine.

If this chakra is fully open and balanced you will feel cosmic union with all - no separation. Life becomes an everlasting expression of divine love and bliss!

If the heart chakra is disharmonious in someone, they expect recognition and constant reassurance in return for the love they give. They may find it hard to receive love and affection. Tenderness and softness make them feel embarrassed. If the heart is completely shut (this is rare) its closure will express itself as coldness, indifference, heartlessness and ruthlessness. In order to feel anything again it may require very strong external stimulation.

KARMIC LESSON: Love

We have learnt, in this life and others, that it is not safe to have an open loving heart. Life is often disappointing, and so we protect ourselves from pain, and also from other people's pain, negativity and fears - so we lose the ability to trust the goodness of life and the cosmos. Sometimes our lives get stuck in a groove of discontent and unhappiness, in particular, we don't trust LOVE and relationships.

On the other hand, as we dare to love again, the more we love, the stronger we become on a spiritual level. Loving makes us spiritually mature and then our spiritual heart can, and does, stay open to love and it attracts love to it from all directions. Through the heart, human beings have tremendous courage and willingness, and even though we may be disappointed time and again, we give love another chance. And another.

Karmic lessons arise from any unresolved past life issue around all matters concerning the heart: love, affection, rejection, jealousy, fear, abandonment, cruelty, manipulation, misuse of love (not sex) for selfish aims, and so on.

Anything that makes you feel truly **heartbroken** can damage the heart chakra; however, on the other hand, being heartbroken (a very interesting use of words) can also ultimately break open the heart chakra and bring immense healing and progress for the soul. The difference between the two lies in the Eleventh Chakra (which is at the edge of your aura beneath your feet) which is connected to the **soul's intention - ask yourself was it my soul's intention to break open my heart in this manner, or through this situation?**

The karmic wounding or pattern that can lie within the heart chakra is "I AM NOT WORTHY TO RECEIVE LOVE" or "I am not good enough to be loved; I am not lovable." This underlying wounding will need to be healed consciously in life, usually by the events of life showing us that we are lovable, and indeed that we are loved. We must 'let it in' to the heart, though.

If this chakra is blocked from past lives the person will often 'play at love' and be incapable of real intimacy, and will resist feeling. They may not be aware that they are doing this, and will think their behaviour is normal. These people act as if everything is FINE, to avoid the truth of their deeper feelings. They will avoid bonding by creating conflicts, tension and drama and then will use this as an excuse to distance themselves. Love becomes a mental exercise, and not a function of the heart chakra. They may also *blame* the other, and yet are co-dependent.

When in our past we have loved unconditionally the heart chakra becomes enriched, full, expansive - the person knows how to love, so life is joy! They love themselves unconditionally (this is not egotism). They have a great passion for life. They take responsibility for themselves and how they feel. They love all and everything, whether it is people, animals, nature, the Universe, or God, for they have heart gnosis (heart wisdom) where the heart knows that All is One and cannot be separated from Love. Inclusivity!

MANTRA: I AM LOVE

To heal and harmonize the underlying karmic pattern of this chakra the mantra is: **I AM LOVE**. This OPENS and transforms the heart into a pulsing loving expression of the divine; old blocked energies are washed away in the light of the divine.

Again, my suggestion is that you try this simple mantra, and see if you can feel a difference; you will need to do this simple exercise for at least **a month** to have lasting results.

Process: Relax, become aware of the Heart Chakra at the front of your body, putting your breath there, breathing in through the front of the chakra and out through the back part of the chakra (which is in the same position only on the back of the body). How does it feel? Be aware of the energy there - if there seems to be no energy there, that is how it is at the moment.

Now, see, sense, or feel the **colour** of your Heart Chakra, after a few minutes say to your Heart Chakra: "I AM LOVE". Repeat the mantra a few times, and relax.

How does it feel in the area of the Heart Chakra, is there any change? any movement, more energy? … more expansion? Note any changes between when you began and after the process. Don't spend time analysing, just do it, feel it, keep trying it and you will get results.

Again, you can walk around all day saying "I AM LOVE" and you will be Love! You will attract love to yourself from every direction, from friends, co-workers, family, the angels, even strangers - for in truth you are love, your Iamness is love.

Don't forget there is a Cosmic Law that says "**we attract what we radiate**" and if you are radiating love you will attract that to you; if you radiate negativity then you will attract that back.

If you feel the fear coming up that relates to this chakra, like feeling unloved or abandoned, or that you are unlovable and isolated, or are judgemental and cold, then say "I AM LOVE" with conviction and see how this instantly helps.

Wearing green or rose pink and saying: "I AM LOVE" will really expand your loving Heart Chakra!!

PRACTICAL HELP FOR THE HEART

Homework: Choose any or all of these simple tools to help open and balance your chakra. I suggest in particular that you bring the colour forcefully into your life for this month.

- **Pink** flowers are especially good for gentle revitalizing and healing of the heart.

- **Wear pink** and/or green for the next month, everyday.

- **Walk** or spend time in nature; this helps the physical heart, etheric body, blood, circulation and brings harmony and peace through the whole being.

- **Open eye meditation:** look at pink sunsets, pink clouds, immerse yourself in any pink in the sky.

- Listen to **love music**; any music that makes you feel strongly, especially sacred music; romantic, classical, etc., whatever is uplifting for you.

- **Dance**, in a circle with others or romantically with a partner.

- **Tone**: 'AH', like a tender sigh. This leads to direct awareness of the heart. *Say it lots* to others! It is the most open sound, all babies make it, it is a universal sound that affects everyone, all nationalities know it.

- **Gems: Rose quartz** for tenderness, gentleness. It envelops the soul in loving vibrations and helps to heal the wounds of the heart. It also helps the soul to give and receive love freely. **Pink tourmaline** expands the heart, and connects to the female expression of divine love. **Emeralds** are all embracing love, and strengthen and deepen love, bringing healing love vibrations from the cosmos to earth. **Jade** brings peace, harmony, fairness, modesty, relaxing the heart, helps with restlessness, and helps to sleep and dream well.

- **Essential oil** of <u>rose</u> - attar of roses. There is no other fragrance that affects the aura like rose does; it harmonizes the entire being. It is the most healing oil, and does beautiful things in the aura and the heart. It brings deep joy and opens you to divine love.

- **Let love** be your aim! (One time that you can 'fake it to make it!') Ask for love to come to you in a perfect way, and that you will recognize it when it does and let it in. Stay 'open to love' this month.

- *Love the unlovable* - in yourself and in others.

- Say **"I AM LOVE!"** lots and lots, every day.

- **Feel intensely** (if only for a month! experiment!) Read poetry, look at art, walk in nature.

- All **Ascended Masters** work through the heart, in particular: Lady Mary, Jesus the Christ (ie Lord Sananda), Lord Buddha, Lady Portia, Lady Nada, Quan Yin. Call upon them, ask to have an experience of that particular Master. Also apply any of these Master Oils on the heart chakra (chest) to have a more profound connection to these Masters and harmonize this chakra (Master oils available through www.cobolt.com.au).

- **Meditate** with hands over the heart and breathe through the heart, feeling it as much as possible. See or feel what colour your heart chakra is.

Throat Chakra Symbol

THROAT CHAKRA
I AM AND I WILL

Colour:	Brilliant sky blue/silver
Element:	Ether
Sense:	Hearing
Symbol:	Circle within a downward pointed triangle within a larger circle
Lotus:	16 petals
Location:	Throat area; front and back of neck
Function:	Communication; self and soul expression; speaking your truth; willpower
Law of Correspondence:	Solar plexus chakra (3rd)

GENERAL:

This, the fifth chakra, is associated with our neck, throat, jaw, ears, voice, bronchia, upper lungs, and thyroid gland. Issues or problems with the thyroid gland are associated with throat chakra wounding.

The main energy of the throat chakra gives us the ability to communicate in a true sense; it also fulfils for us the function of self expression, the ability to Speak our Truth. It is the main area which holds willpower; which, basically, means that it governs the will required to translate things into action.

The energy of the throat chakra is very fine; indeed, as we move upwards through the body, the energies of the chakras become finer and finer. The throat chakra is very vulnerable to external influences. It is a tiny area, with little protection on a physical level, as there is no large muscle in this area, and so it can be easily damaged; if exposed to draughts, for instance, or sudden temperature changes. Often we tuck our chin in if we feel vulnerable in this area. The nape of the neck (which is the back part of the chakra) is also vulnerable, being the place most open to psychic attack - when we talk about the 'devil being on my back' we are referring to this.

The throat chakra is very important, it is a bridge. Without the throat chakra, we would be unable to express our individuality; we could not share our soul, our thoughts or feelings. We use the throat chakra as a speaking voice to express ourselves, but this area is also responsible for any other kind of expression, including those of our soul levels. So our use of colour, gesture, dance, movement, the written word - all these use the energy of the throat chakra as an organ of communication of our soul. This does not include idle gossip or 'chit chat', which are not communication in the proper sense, but are just 'noise'.

The throat chakra is strengthened and enriched each time we express ourselves in Truth and with integrity. The easiest way to stimulate this chakra is to do anything with WORDS: speak, lecture, act, chant, write, do journal work, read or write or recite poetry, and - the very best thing to open the throat chakra - SING! It acts as a bridge between our feelings, centred in the heart chakra, and our thoughts, focused in the third eye chakra - through the throat chakra we give voice to our feelings.

Emotion floods the throat chakra, and if it is left unexpressed it stagnates and blocks the throat, and it is as if we cannot *get it out*. It is through this chakra that we express everything alive within us.

Ether is the medium of sound; the medium of the spoken word as well as the Divine word. Ether is also defined as *akasha*, which is the light where all the events, actions, thoughts and feelings of individuals and world events are recorded. It is the throat chakra that draws the vibration and energy of this very fine level into you.

We can reach the deepest levels of knowing and feeling through the throat chakra. Having a balanced and open throat will give us an inner sense of boundlessness - we feel expansive and open like the boundless blue sky. Deep levels and deep calm can be reached by meditating under the blue sky, (or imagining it). Often people with throat chakra problems will fear open spaces - a fear of boundlessness - they want to feel enclosed to feel safe.

This chakra also affects your ears: the more open this chakra is the more you can listen with your soul to the inner voice of God, and to the soul voices of others, with truly receptive hearing; you also know when to be silent.

An open throat chakra speaks the truth. When you lie, it diminishes your soul. (A mucky green slimy-sludge comes oozing out of your aura when you lie.) Inner honesty towards self and others is shown in an upright posture.

When you tell people your truth and express your soul and other people do not value it, this also detracts from your soul. You need to be very strong in your throat and solar plexus to withstand others' opinions, otherwise you will be vulnerable to the negativity directed towards you, you will take it in. Ultimately, we must develop the throat to such a degree that we are strong enough to withstand others' opinions and energy, and we are free to express honestly *regardless!* Therefore, if you are expressing your soul to hundreds or thousands or millions of people, it is really developing your throat chakra! As we know, generally people fear public speaking even more than death!

It is very important to only speak when you are moved to speak! If you're not moved, don't speak. Your body tells you when you need to speak up - you may have a pounding heart, shaking, sweaty palms and so on - when you feel these *you know you have to speak.* At that moment of truth, the spiritual forces are with you, so SAY it! If you miss that moment, then *don't* say it, the moment has passed; you will have to wait for the next opportunity, because if you miss the moment then you won't be heard, or you will be misunderstood. There *will* be another opportunity.

Opening the throat chakra, particularly for women, is not easy. Many women have their whole lives controlled by their throat chakra; it is so poorly functioning that they struggle to express themselves. The reason that women have throat chakra issues is that patriarchal authority has, in the past, conspired to keep it blocked, because people with an open throat chakra **cannot be controlled**.

Traditionally, males have been the oppressor, the one with the VOICE in the world, while females have been the oppressed. But in this model of the patriarchal society both males and females have been living in self-limiting roles. This is the area that women are working on most at the moment - it is only in the last hundred years that most women were allowed to vote, that is, were given a voice in the world.

A woman may often feel that there is an inner roadblock constructed in her throat - as the throat tries to open, memories of previous 'blocking' tend to rise up within, causing even more constriction. Usually, this inner pain originates from many previous lives as a female in which the soul has experienced pain, torture and death for speaking out. So it is that original fear which rises up again and chokes her, panic sets in, and eventually there comes a feeling that she will die if she does speak up and will die if she doesn't! Women need to express who they are, and find a voice in the world, and at the moment the spiritual forces are pushing them to do this.

A goddess is a female with an open throat chakra! She is in her power and cannot be controlled.

If a person is 'cut off' at the throat area then there is little flow of energy from the head to the body, and vice versa. This can mean that the person can be all 'in the head', as we say, or all in the body. This can also result in their language being coarse, blunt, blatant, cool or businesslike, as the heart chakra energy (love and feeling) doesn't flood the voice. If this area is disharmonious, then whenever you try to express your deeper thoughts and feelings, you get a 'lump' in your throat, and your force may drain away, or your voice sound forced.

KARMIC LESSONS: Communication and Expressing Soul

There are many past life issues here, creating karmic issues that have to do with fear related to speaking, expressing or writing one's truth. These unresolved issues arise are because people have been suppressed, abused, tortured just for being themselves; for instance, being oppressed for being a gypsy, being Jewish, or being a woman. We have very painful memories of being tortured for expressing our truth stuck in our throat chakras; especially memories of the tongue being cut out, and being burnt at the stake. It can take many lifetimes to recover from our experiences of fighting for Truth, so we often avoid it. If this has been your experience in a previous life and you have suffered for it, then you may have earned the spiritual title of "Defender of the Truth".

Also, if in the past you have been a member of a Silent Order, a hermit, a mystic, someone perhaps suppressing their voice in the name of religion or spiritual practice, you will face challenges on the throat chakra level.

There will also be challenges if you have used your voice and the power of words in any life in order to manipulate others. Great orators can use their open throat chakras for the highest good or equally for great destruction; Hitler's use of oratory is an example of the misuse of the power of the throat chakra.

The underlying negative karmic pattern that is held in the throat chakra is "I MUST BE QUIET AND GOOD". Or: "If I talk a lot no-one will notice that I am too scared to express my real self."

If in the past a person has been wounded on the level of the throat chakra then they try to hide their true self, are silenced by shame, live in self-hurt. They will not express their feelings, especially those of anger, frustration, hurt, love; this leads to their being depressed, with limited self-expression, being closed off, not wanting to express the sorrow or anger they feel, whether it originates in this life or a previous one. They may feel it is safer to hide in silence than to say anything; or they may hide behind jokes, not allowing silence. The person with deep wounding in the throat chakra, or total blockage there, will lie to protect themself - which is damaging to the soul integrity, and limits the free flow of creative energy and awareness. Often they turn to self and substance abuse in order to numb the spirit - with food, alcohol, music, drugs.

When you are blocked in the throat chakra and not expressing yourself your life force is very weak; so for good health it is necessary to express yourself! When we suppress our self, that energy implodes into our entire being; you keep swallowing it down, pushing it deeper down into the psyche. When you are just starting more consciously to express who you are, it can be awkward, it can come out wrong, you might have tantrums and suchlike; but that's OK, you are still learning! Just keep going with a clear intention to speak with love and truth, and it will clear up. The noises that may come out of you are the ones that you wanted to make at the time of the original injury (lifetimes ago).

Neck problems abound! We have tense, crooked shoulders, spasms, throat problems, voice problems, and so on. Blocked emotion has to manifest sometime, the body cannot contain it forever. The Silent Child needs love. It has been prevented from speaking its truth, has been told to be quiet and be good, and it has swallowed its joy. Self-pity comes from not being listened to, or not being believed.

To whom do you need to say something that so far has been unexpressed? Say it aloud, if possible to the person concerned, or visualize them in front of you and say it. Did your parents encourage you to speak truth and express yourself as a child?

Very many of us, women in particular, are being urgently called now in the 21st Century to harmonize the throat chakra - there is a 'hurry on' to unblock this chakra; so that we are not cut off at the neck, but everything is connected and flowing dynamically. The reason for the urgency with this chakra is that it represents the archetype of the Aquarian Age; the new consciousness which we are endeavouring to embrace and become. The open throat chakra represents the future, the communication age: email, mobile phones, intelligent machines, global learning, mass media, the worldwide web, communication satellites and so on. We now have the means for very quick, clear, direct communication. Technology has given us the World, in seconds. The potential for connection with others has expanded phenomenally - 'as within, so without' - so we are all being called to open our throat chakras to enter into the Aquarian Age, and become the Communicator. It is the time to speak up, be heard, find your voice, do your thing! This is the masculine side of the throat chakra; the feminine side would be to release the divine goddess within and let her roar! ... or purr, perhaps!

If you have developed this chakra in your previous lives then you will speak from your inner core with clear intention. You will have respect for the written and spoken word, know the power of words, never gossip or criticise. Your words are healing and uplifting; they speak from the heart, fully connected with the energy of heart and throat chakras.

Of course, we can have great power in our voice that commands awe and respect; we may have the Divine in our voice which often makes an extraordinary singer. This is usually a spiritual gift, given because of past lives in which we have sacrificed our life for the evolution or succour of others, using our voice or through the written word. An example of this which I have 'seen' through the Akashic Records is a client of mine who in a previous life was singing in a choir in a cathedral; the cathedral suddenly came under attack from anti-religious forces of the time. As the parishioners, who were at prayer, were brutally beaten by the attackers, a lone member of the choir stood up in the gallery and instead of running for his life like the others, started singing a heavenly hymn. This valiant act helped the souls leave their physical bodies (those that had been slain); it helped ease the transition of these souls from this world to the next, which help they needed because the souls had not been prepared for death as they would have been in less traumatic circumstances.

MANTRA: I AM AND I WILL

To heal and harmonize the underlying karmic pattern of this chakra the mantra is: **I AM AND I WILL**. Chanting this will open the throat so that the head energies are fully connected and flowing with the body energies. You will feel serene, yet more powerful.

Again, my suggestion is, as with each of the chakras, you try this simple mantra, and see if you can feel a difference; you will need to do this simple exercise for at least **a month** to have lasting results.

Process: Relax, become aware of the Throat Chakra at the front of your body, putting your breath there, breathing in through the front of the chakra and out through the back part of the chakra (at the back of the neck). How does it feel? Be aware of the energy there - if there seems to be no energy there, that is how it is at the moment.

Now, see, sense, or feel the **colour** of your Throat Chakra, and after a few minutes say to your Throat Chakra: "I AM AND I WILL". Repeat the mantra a few times, and relax.

How does it feel in the area of the Throat Chakra, is there any change? ...any movement, more energy? … more expansion? Note any changes between when you began and after the process; don't spend time analysing, just do it, feel it, keep on trying it and you will get results.

Wearing clear blue and saying: "I AM AND I WILL" will help you express what is in your soul, and you will dance and sing!

PRACTICAL HELP FOR THE THROAT CHAKRA

Homework: Choose any or all of these simple tools to help open and balance your chakra. I suggest in particular that you bring the colour forcefully into your life for this month.

- **Wear sky blue**, bright blues. Do **not** wear navy if possible, and definitely not near the throat. (Navy is the colour of a closed and blocked throat - 'uniforms' are often navy, which represents control and lack of individualism.)

- **Open eye meditation:** Lie on the ground outside, and open the throat, breathe into it, through it, get lost in the sky, then ask for a message from the Divine. Even better is to look at the blue sky over blue water; this frees emotions and feelings, the waves make you aware of 'hidden stuff' and then it's easier to release it.

- Sound therapy, plus any **music** rich in high tones, Angels' music, boundless soaring music.

- **SING!!** This is the best way to open the throat. Singing puts joy to the words of the heart. Get into chanting, acting, speaking, writing, poetry, journal work, etc. These are all finding and expressing your voice.

- **Sound:** "Eh!" (as in Italian exclamation) repeat it like a mantra.

- **Listen** to the sounds of nature, listen to silence, especially *listen to others with your soul.*

- **Stones:** Put aquamarine, turquoise, sapphire, anything blue, in your aura.

- **Essential oils: sage**, (loosens the throat and helps express inner messages from the soul), and **eucalyptus**, (clears and widens the throat, opens us to our inner voice and natural communication).

- **Mantra yoga.**

- **Ascended Master: Archangel Michael** carries the Sword of Truth, and he demands Truth! **Apply this Master Oil on your throat chakra to have a more profound connection to this Master and to harmonize this chakra.**

- Put your truth into **action**! Choose something, and do it in the next month.

- **Speak your truth,** especially at those 'opportune' times. It will empower you.
- **Say what you mean.** "No" means no. "Yes" means yes. (The reason that speech evolved was to say "No"). Say "NoNoNoNo" over and over to remove anger.
- Practice **speaking lower**, let your voice 'drop into your chest', and speak 'lower'.
- Try expressing yourself in **a new way!** Something different.
- An **exercise:** loosen your mouth, let the jaw hang free, put a hand on your belly, and let out a low primeval, wordless noise; grunting, groaning, moaning, rasping etc. -sounds release energy stuck in the throat, and get rid of emotions unexpressed from long ago. (Doing this may connect you to all kinds of feelings, and bring insight into the blockages or you may just feel good to get these noises *out* of your system.)

Third Eye/Brow Chakra Symbol

THIRD EYE/BROW CHAKRA
I AM AND I KNOW

Colour:	Violet/Indigo/Yellow
Element:	Light
Sense:	Sixth sense
Symbol:	The eye
Lotus:	96 petals
Location:	Centre of forehead just above brows at the front, and going out at the back of the head
Function:	Conscious perception of being; seat of higher mental powers; seat of higher clairvoyance
Law of Correspondence:	Sacral chakra (2nd)

GENERAL:

This chakra, the sixth, affects the face, eyes, nose, sinuses, head, skull and scalp, central nervous system, and pituitary gland, (which governs all other glands and hormone production).

As the name suggests, the harmonious functioning of this chakra gives us a third eye, an inner eye, that enables in us a conscious perception of who we are, the realization that we are a being, and allows us to know consciously that we *exist*. The more open it is, the more conscious you are of your beingness - your total being on a physical and all other levels.

It is the seat of higher mental powers, intelligent discernment, knowledge and mind power. It can be over-stimulated easily; it is of very fine, high, subtle vibrations. For most people it is not as easy to relate to as the other chakras are. It gives the ability to understand non-physical things, abstract concepts, intuition, clairvoyance, dreaming, out-of-body sight, magical awareness, inner knowing, and enables experiences of the non-physical realms. This chakra *locates* you in the non-solid realms and other dimensions.

For the third eye chakra to become open and remain open, we must have good grounding in the base chakra and sacral chakra, otherwise, we may be subject to insanity, hysteria, panic attacks. Many people want to be clairvoyant ('clear seeing'), clairaudient ('clear hearing'), or clairsentient ('clear feeling'); but when you are clairvoyant you see *everything that's there*. You don't just see all the beautiful celestial beings, you see all the dark, negative stuff as well. So don't be in too much of a hurry - let it develop in its own time, so that you are ready to see everything without being knocked off centre or afraid. It *will* develop in its own time, and it will connect you to other dimensions and the unseen worlds when you are ready.

This chakra is developing more quickly now, as more and more people are able to think for themselves, are more grounded, and have the integrity and responsibility needed to have an open third eye. Over the next few years (until 2010-2012) we will experience a lot of softening in the third eye area and in the etheric body, and in general we will experience our intuition, our inner guidance and the unseen, more readily. We need to trust it. This development bodes well for humanity and our future, and is a necessary step in our evolution.

When your third eye is fully open and functioning well you are enlightened! You are fully lit up from deep inside. You *just know*. You see everything and you understand. We are all using our third eye to some degree already.

There is a change in reality when your consciousness expands and this chakra is opening. Whenever your sense of reality is changing, you may experience sensations of dizziness, as you get used to the new level of reality. You may feel a sense of disorientation, clumsiness, otherworldliness. These are all normal and it is not uncommon to experience phases of these things. Also, you may feel weird sensations in the eyes, or pain or pressure in the third eye region. (Please always get yourself checked out by your medical practitioner, your doctor or naturopath or kinesiologist or homeopath, just to make sure there's nothing physically wrong with you - don't assume the sensations are *only* a spiritual phenomenon.)

Your dream world becomes rich and meaningful, and your intuition and imagination are more active; the invisible worlds are more accessible, and you will generate lots of ideas. Because your third eye is connected to the sacral chakra, when it opens it may affect your creativity. Dreams become more prophetic and play a greater role in guiding our lives as we understand them more in the future.

As we move into the Aquarian Age, it is becoming vital to develop the third eye area which connects us to our inner world. We need to have a strong inner core that is peaceful in order to withdraw into it, and to find inner peace to protect us from the outer world, which is increasingly busy, active, frenetic, bombarding us with constant energy and information overload. We will have to go deep inside to our inner core to feel *freedom*.

When we worry, this stresses the third eye chakra. Our natural instinct is to rub the brow when we're trying to work something out...in this automatic gesture we are trying to stimulate the third eye to give us greater vision, greater clarity. When we worry too much and are going up and down those endless mental tram tracks that go nowhere it causes depletion of the third eye chakra energy; we generally feel worn out, and there is never any resolution! *You cannot solve a problem or issue by the same consciousness in which you created it.* You need to go up, or sideways, in consciousness to resolve it; you need to find a new way of looking at it, achieve a new level of understanding, get another perspective. The best way of going sideways in consciousness is to go outside! Walk, run, move in nature - it is not possible to do the 'tram track' thinking when you are active outside. The energy of the third eye will settle when you are 'outside' and then the answers can come, with an "Ah ha! Now I've got it!"

Sometimes the third eye chakra is **yellow**, signifying rational thought. Practical or logical thought is brownish yellow. There is nothing wrong with this, but balance needs to be there to bring in the other side of the brain, and then **indigo** appears in the third eye chakra; this is for elevated thoughts, and intuition. **Violet** is the highest level of vibration at the third eye level, giving us the divine thought, and true clairvoyance.

Very few people have a completely open third eye chakra; these are the highly advanced souls or enlightened beings.

If the third eye is harmonious in you, and active to some degree, then you are intelligent, you can think laterally, philosophically, imaginatively, conceptually, intuitively, vividly. You will be open to mystical insight, have a good ability to visualize, and the potential for original thought (which is so very rare...!) This enlivens your access to dreams, insight, intuition - when this chakra is in harmony, you can see beyond the physical realm to the Divine in everything. You are aware of subtleties, and endless worlds between the material world and the world of Pure Being.

As it opens *collectively*, people at large will come to perceive the world differently and develop unlimited thinking.

When the third eye is disharmonious, then the person's energy is often drawn up into the head. This is especially so in western countries; our auras are often top heavy, out of balance; we become too spiritual and not grounded, or else we are thinking too much, we are too mental and not in our bodies.

Often people who pull their energy up to their head are inclined to ignore their physical bodies. They have what I call 'unrealised' bodies: they are skinny, pasty skinned, with big heads, and look physically under-developed even as an adult. They are not holistic, they always want things to be proved, and over-analyse. They try to use the force of the mind to convince you, and enjoy logical, rational arguments as if they are the only truth...! They don't grasp the truth or deeper meaning of anything that they feel or see inside themselves; things like dreams, intuition, messages and so on. They are out of touch with themselves, and therefore everyone else. They reject spiritual truth, therefore they don't understand those who are anchored in it and devoted to it. They lack vision, the capacity to see the bigger, deeper picture. Yet they can still be very active and intelligent with good mental faculties; they can also be very muddled, vague, and have fuzzy thinking.

All these aspects are a misuse of the beautiful energies of the third eye chakra, and need to be balanced and harmonized.

KARMIC LESSONS: Going Beyond and Being an Individual

Past life lessons held in this chakra that may damage or wound this chakra, will be to do with the mind, intuition, clairvoyance, and original thought. People have often been punished for being clairvoyant, so their third eye chakra has closed in defence; particularly those who were locked up in asylums, and tortured by the Inquisition, or burnt at the stake. Because you remember these things on a soul level, and you don't want to be tortured again for being clairvoyant, you close down this aspect of your third eye. But, at some stage, your soul has to realize that it won't be punished again for being clairvoyant, so you will be challenged to open it again; this can be done slowly and gradually, over lifetimes, so that you get used to having this third eye consciousness again.

Many old Atlantean souls are incarnating or gathering again now, in Australia and America; many of these people (not everyone) will be challenged to open their third eye chakra again, and to heal the old karma from that time in Atlantis*. At the time of the fall of Atlantis, there was a great misuse of the third eye powers, such as mind control, experiments on humans, use of substances to create automatons, and other abuses, and this resulted in a psychic war between the good people (light) and the negative people (dark) at that time. Any issues of mind control, psychic battles, illegal drug problems, and the misuse of clairvoyant abilities will create karma and close this chakra. Misusing clairvoyance for one's own selfish gain, such as to obtain excessive money, power, or influence, will cause karmic dysfunction. There is nothing wrong with using one's clairvoyance and charging money for it, as long as it is a fair exchange, but it is vital not to misuse this gift.

If you have misused your gifts, particularly your third eye energies, then they will be taken away from you. They will only be given back when you have been through tremendous pain and testing, many challenges, once again to prove your integrity, pure intention, and responsibility. When you are deemed pure enough in your intention, and light enough to have the gifts and use them wisely, then they are slowly given back to you. Sometimes people are desperate to have this chakra open, as they have experienced an open third eye before, but

---

* **Note**: Detailed information on Atlantis is available on www.cobolt com.au

because they have committed a misuse they have lost the ability, and it causes them great pain, and they yearn for it.

The underlying karmic pattern held in the chakra that you may bring in with you is "IT'S JUST MY IMAGINATION, WHAT DO I KNOW?" or 'I must be mad ... to think that ..."

If this chakra is unbalanced in its development then it will be obvious in different, even contradictory, ways. For instance, if the emphasis in this and previous lives has been solely on the intellect, and the person has been an academic, a scientist, a doctor, a scholar or professor, then this aspect of the third eye chakra can become overdeveloped to the detriment of the soul. Then they tend to theorise about everything, are very dry, with much book learning, are usually thin, and humourless. They are not dynamically in tune with what's going on. They use control to avoid feeling and intuition. They are restricted in their capacity to experience joy. Often very opinionated, they don't trust their experiences, and want everything to be explained logically, rationally. They have a body full of tension because it's not given enough attention. They also have an urge which requires everything to be perfect in order for them to be happy...

How much do you live in your mind? It is important to think for yourself. Can you at times go against what society and others think you 'should' do? When you trust your own experience, you start to live by an inner set of rules in accordance with the universal laws. You then pulse with the cosmic pulse! *You have **lifetimes** of learning within you, now is the time to access this learning through the sixth chakra.*

On the converse side, if this chakra is not functioning well in a person, or is blocked or even closed, they may feel stupid, and unable to think for themselves or to make their own decisions.

When the third eye is open, balanced and the energies are moving beautifully then this person is someone we notice in the crowd, there is something indefinable about them, different, special. Mysterious. These people often become what we call pioneers, leaders in their field of endeavour, whether this is science, or ballet, or government; Albert Enstein is a good example of this, with his third eye open he pioneered science in a new direction, and still does.

As we journey through our lives we generally learn from our varied experiences, and by this gain a deeper knowing, wisdom. This helps the third eye chakra to develop in a healthy way and we begin to trust more and more in our own inner vision and guidance.

Eventually, we become our own inner mystic, seeing the goodness in others, have great patience, and understand that we are not 'on our own'. Those with a well developed third eye chakra know their part in the cosmic picture, and understand that each experience is for their highest good, even when it is painful. They have wisdom and vision. They know the sacred and holy place inside themselves. They know that those who are *not* in touch with this core are living under illusion, and they have compassion for ignorance.

They are visionaries, far-seeing, and are often drawn to teaching and empowering others to become who they really are. They are full of hope and hold the light for humanity.

MANTRA: I AM AND I KNOW

To heal and harmonize the underlying karmic pattern of this chakra the mantra is: **I AM AND I KNOW.**

Again, my suggestion is that you try this simple mantra, and see if you can feel a difference; you will need to do this simple exercise regularly for at least a **month** to have lasting results.

Process: Relax, become aware of the Brow Chakra at the front of your head, putting your breath there, breathing in through the front of the chakra and out through the back part of the chakra (at the back of your head). How does it feel? Be aware of the energy there - if there seems to be no energy there, that is how it is at the moment.

Now, see, sense, or feel the **colour** of your Brow Chakra, and after a few minutes say to your Brow Chakra: "I AM AND I KNOW". Repeat the mantra a few times, and relax.

Note any changes between when you began and after the process; again, don't spend time analysing, just do it, feel it, keep trying it. You will get results.

If you feel fear associated with the Brow Chakra, like the fear of putting your life purpose into action, or a fear of being clairvoyant and 'seeing' the unseen, or fear of standing out and being different, being yourself, an individual, then by saying "I AM AND I KNOW" you will come back to yourself and be enabled to fulfil the purpose for which you incarnated, and to progress as an individual and to be yourself. *The most spiritual thing you can do is to be the most YOU that you can be - its that easy and that hard.*

Wearing violet or purples and saying: "I AM AND I KNOW" will help you express your Higher Self, and your higher consciousness.

(When we say I AM AND I KNOW, we say this in all humility; we do not come from arrogance. It is *not* that "I know more than you, so I am better than you", it is in the sense of "I know because I experience the unknown and this is a very humbling experience, and a great honour.")

PRACTICAL HELP FOR THE THIRD EYE

Homework: Choose any or all of these simple tools to help open and balance your chakra. I suggest in particular that you bring the colour forcefully into your life for this month.

- **Wear** purple, or violet.

- **Violet** flowers around to purify, gain clarity, heal, stimulate and strengthen the third eye.

- **Open eyed meditation:** the deep blue night sky and stars. This opens the mind and the third eye to the boundless expanse of all manifestation. It gives you a sense of subtler planes beyond the stars - there are infinite spiritual worlds out there. Let the stars speak to you!

- **Music:** anything relaxing that evokes feelings of cosmic consciousness, and inner soaring. JS Bach is good for harmonizing the third eye.

- **Tone:** "eeeeee". This takes you upward for inspiration.

- **Gems: lapis lazuli** makes your soul feel safe in the cosmos. It is the priestess stone used in ordinations in ancient Egypt. Stick it on your third eye! It takes the mind inward, stimulates clairvoyance and intuition. **Blue sapphire** opens the mind to cosmic knowing, transforms the body and soul. It is the bridge between the infinite and the finite.

- **Essential oils:** the **mint** family dissolves blockages in the third eye and rids the self of old confining thought patterns. **Jasmine** opens us to visions of higher truths, links the third eye with the heart. Other (less powerful) oils are violet, hyacinth, rose geranium.

- **Meditation**, visualization, ponderings, daydreams are all important for the third eye; this month do as much as possible of these activities and *waste time* (without guilt!!)

- **Jnana yoga:** focus on the Absolute, meditate on God.

- Ascended Masters: St Germain, Pallas Athene, Radiant One - **put any of these Master Oils on the third eye** area.

- **Breathe** into this area in through the front, out through the back, observe the colour and feelings.

- **Let go** of limited thinking!! Pretend if you have to, but think unlimited, infinite, boundless, creative thoughts.
- Follow your **intuition**: it is your best friend. It will lead you to your bliss, trust it, follow it and go with it. (In-tuition: inner teaching, inside knowing.)
- **Tune in** - take the time to ask the big questions this month.
- **Eat Purple** foods.
- Defocus your eyes and **look at auras** (of your friends and people you are close to).
- **Rub the third eye** and make the 'eeeeee' tone, then meditate and, or, do aura viewing.
- **Don't overdo it!** If it feels tense, painful, relax and let it be.

CROWN CHAKRA
I AM THAT I AM

Colour:	**White, opalescent**
Element:	**None**
Sense:	**None**
Symbol:	**1,000 petalled lotus or the rose**
Lotus:	**1,000 petalled lotus**
Location:	**Top of the head**
Function:	**Seat of highest human perfection and purest being. Connection with the Divine.**
Law of Correspondence:	**Base Chakra (1st)**

GENERAL:

The Crown is different in its structure and energy to the other main chakras. Within the crown chakra are four spinning gateways, each with a flat spinning vortex. The crown is connected to the pineal gland in the body. It is both the most simple and yet complex chakra.

This, the seventh chakra, is the seat of highest human perfection, and purest being. It is the place where we started our journey into life, and we will return to it at the end of our development.

The main function of the crown chakra is to enable unity with our own divinity, as well as with the greater divinity, the source of all things, GOD. When this opens, your energy field becomes one with the whole universe and you experience a very high state of consciousness. When the crown opens it acts like a magnet drawing you up towards the divine, and at the same time pulling you down into the physical. The physical body is the temple of the divine and deserves to be adored as such. The more your physical body fills with divine energy, the more you will adore and worship your physical body in a balanced way, and not treat it as a tool of your ego.

This spiritual centre, the crown chakra, contains the energy of all your spiritual practices, meditations, prayers, devotion, spiritual conscience, spiritual purpose and beauty. Also, that feeling of 'divine discontent' is located here. When the achievements of the external world no longer feel particularly fulfilling, and when what may have given us joy or contentment in the past doesn't do so any more, and we feel the deepest yearning for something, yet we know not what...this is 'divine discontent'. It is a healthy discontent, for it leads you forward.

The crown chakra is your centre of your highest spiritual quest or purpose, your highest truths, the deepest meanings of your life and your existence. This is the centre of the beauty of existence. It is from here that you ask God for answers. When it opens, you receive revelations from your own higher self, your inner divinity, and you achieve self-realization.

The crown is a receptor for incoming stellar energies! It unites the highest levels of your self with the body-mind and the Earth.

When it unfolds, any blockages remaining in other chakras dissolve. It unfolds in layers, at a number of levels. It is an exquisitely fine, high vibration here - there are no blockages in the crown chakra - there can be no blockage between you and God. The Crown is closed or it is open to a certain degree. Because there are no blockages in the energy of the Crown chakra there is also no karmic pattern held within the Crown chakra.

When it starts to open more you might feel as though you are waking from a long dream, and after this you experience everyday reality very differently. You may feel a great sense of inner spaciousness, or of emptiness, which is identical to the greatest sense of abundance - as you are an empty chalice ready to be filled to overflowing with Love from the Divine! (The sense of boundlessness is first experienced at the throat chakra; this feeling expands up through the other chakras as you continue the journey.)

Sometimes when the Crown chakra begins to be more active, it feels as though the bones of the skull are lifting up and out slightly, and that there is a volcano underneath! Or it may feel as though the top of your head is sliced off, or is very sore. In some cases the bones do actually shift and the shape of your head changes slightly, even as an adult.

A baby's fontanelle (which means 'fountain', and is the soft spot on the top of their head) remains open between 9-24 months of age, which means they stay very connected to God. The spiritual forces are still very strong and close to you as an infant. The first memory you have is when you really started to be here on earth, when the spiritual forces are lifting away from you, to enable the soul to accept its life here on earth. The fontanelle closes when the soul is ready. It is best for us to be connected and open to the spiritual forces for as long as possible, in order to anchor the Divine deep within us. Babies are not separated from God, they are in Bliss.

If the crown is closed, there is no God consciousness or spiritual awareness; no understanding of spirituality. There may be despair, a lack of purpose, a sense of life being meaningless, a great fear of death, energy disorders such as chronic exhaustion, anxiety, depression, (there are also many other reasons for these disorders). All of this prevents you from connecting to your higher levels.

When the crown chakra is fully open, it emits a vast aura of light that radiates for miles and affects everyone around, it is uplifting and healing. This light is depicted as a halo in religious texts and paintings. The halo usually indicates ascension, (or at least a very pure radiant soul).

We are living in an age of profound disconnection from God and our divine nature. The mass consciousness experiences fear of being connected to the earth and fear of being connected to God. So most people feel stuck in between the two, feeling that they are 'lost in space', with no understanding of it all. Because of this disconnection, people resort to self-abuse, addictions to drugs, alcohol, sex, food, overwork, and so on - generally, they grasp at anything that gives a superficial, artificial, 'high'. It is an interesting word we use when we say we are 'high'; for it is really the 'high' of God that we seek, the heights of Bliss, or an ecstatic union with the divine. But we try to get there without any effort, living in an instant-consciousness; we want it instantly! Even if we have spiritual experiences while on drugs it is only a glimpse that we see; a door opens to another reality, but access is never sustained. Trying to do this through drugs can retard your evolution, and repeated use of 'mind-altering' drugs makes holes in your aura.

If the crown chakra is not open, or is only slightly open, then a person may have a high degree of success in the world, with material success and possessions, and may think that they are totally in control of their life, but they will still feel like an 'orphan'. They feel empty, cut-off, isolated, and not able to reach out to others. This may create in them an over-proud, narcissistic, ungrateful, self-important attitude, resistant to self-development. They may be separated from their true core, or have a core that is frozen.

Since they don't acknowledge any power outside themselves or any divine influence, they can't ask for guidance or help. To them, nothing is higher than themselves! No-one is worth asking! They can be very conscious, creative, alert, intelligent - but are missing anything from 'beyond'. They are harsh on their own physical body, unfeeling towards others' illnesses; seeing every illness or emotion as a sign of weakness. They impose their will on everyone else, constantly trying to control. If this attitude stays stuck then the crown will remain closed until death.

They need to open to other ways of being, and loosen their attitudes. Sometimes they can be religious leaders whose connection to God is very dogmatic, experiencing the divine only through books, dogmas, scriptures; but He is not a living presence within their heart.

A closed crown chakra means the person generally has a limited tolerance of other people, especially of their differences - and so is limited and identifies as *being* their age, gender, colour, success, wealth, or status.

The aim of course is to have all seven of the chakras open, bright, and functioning dynamically, which would enable us to CELEBRATE THE DIFFERENCES instead of trying to destroy the differences.

The more our crown chakra opens the more mastery we have. We become the Master; the inner guru or mystic archetype is strong within us. It knows joy, bliss, mastery, oneness, universal love.

Mastery over one's physical body = good health and vitality.

Mastery over one's emotions = stability and health.

Mastery over one's mind = serenity and peace.

The master in you knows that all is love. It does not seek external power because the real power is in being your true self, and knowing your true self. You don't have to prove anything to anyone, just be yourself. Often those living with a developed crown chakra will help, teach, and empower others to see their own inner master, their inner divinity, and to become their own source of highest wisdom. To do this requires a high degree of love and complete acceptance of who they are.

Most people would rather go to a teacher or guru and be offered enlightenment than do it themselves. Others go to a guru, or follow a religion because they will not claim the God or guru within, thinking that is sinful or blasphemous, or not wanting to be responsible for themselves. It is appropriate at points of our development to learn from others, to devote yourself to another for learning. It is not necessary, or even appropriate, to devote yourself forever to a particular lineage or guru. We learn from all traditions, all teachers; learning from every source of wisdom over the course of our incarnations to become whole human beings.

There are some great beings on the planet now - they are doing great things. Learn from what they are teaching, but do not give away your power to them. Do not assume that you could never be like them. When your crown is crowned (crown chakra fully open) you let go of everything that is *not yourself*. You let go of anything that limits your beauty, intelligence, wisdom, creativity, abundance, brilliance, radiance. Then you illuminate your being with wonder and delight! Enlightenment can come from a very simple life; a simple existence can lead you to greatness.

edge of aura

4

3

2

1

6 inches

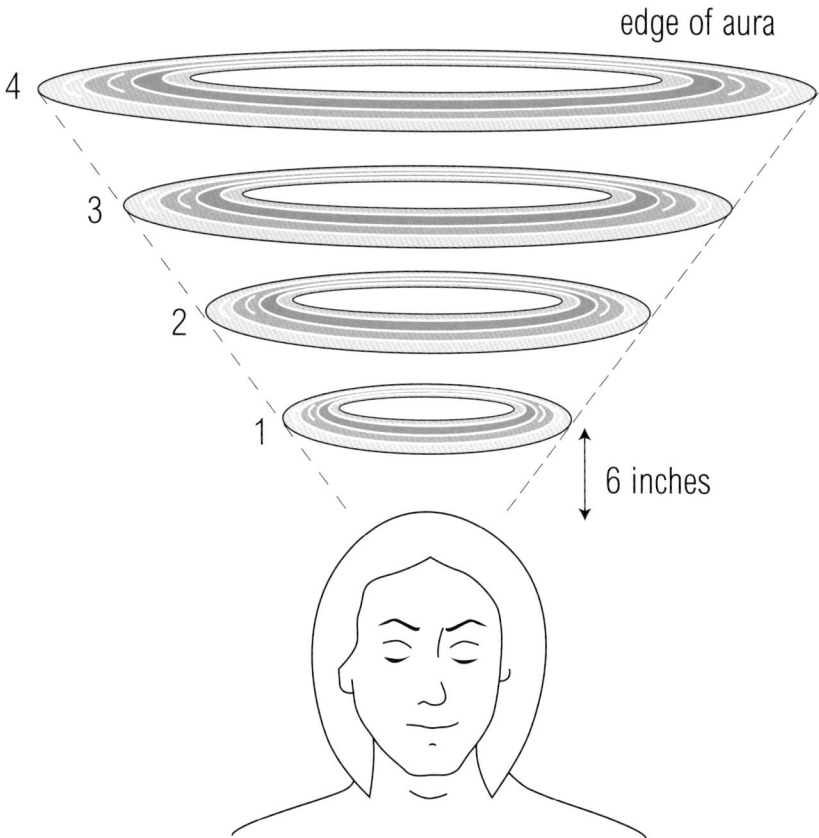

1. Soul self / overself = soul
2. Star self = 4th dimension
3. Universal self = 5th dimension
4. Galaxy self = our galaxy

4 "Gates" of Crown Chakra

FOUR GATES OF THE CROWN CHAKRA

Each gate is like a flat spinning vortex or wheel of energy that, when functioning, will connect you to different experiences and realities.

First level:	*6" above the head is the Soul Star*
Second level:	**12" above the head is the Star Gateway**
Third level:	*18" above the head is the Universal Gateway*
Fourth level:	**24" above the head is the Galactic Gateway**

Soul Star symbolizes where your soul is at now - it is a picture of your Overself. The symbol held there may be current for months, years or lifetimes. This level contains your spiritual conscience and practices.

Star Gateway is your connection to spiritual light forces, and it is through here that you can ground their energies into your being. Blessings come in through here.

Universal Gateway connects you to the fifth dimension, which is the Universal aspect of being. All is one; no separation. Everything and everyone else is one with me, and we are all one with God. Here you can merge fully with Bliss.

Galaxy Gateway is different to the other gateways; it connects us to the galaxy. Cosmic star energies come in through here, allowing you to connect to other planets and stars. Astrological influences come in here. This gate can be open even when the others are not. It is at the outer edge of your aura.

PRACTICAL HELP FOR THE CROWN

Homework: Choose any or all of these simple tools to help open and balance your chakra. I suggest in particular that you bring the colour forcefully into your life for this month.

- **Wear white** all month.

- White **flowers** around to open you to divine light, knowledge and healing.

- **Open eyed meditation:** time spent alone on a mountain peak if possible; this is the best way to open the crown. (Think of all the holy men that live up high, on mountains, or have their retreats there.)

- **Music:** silence. In silence you start to hear the fullness present in the silence, you may even hear the cosmic 'aum' that sounds unceasingly. Any music that prepares you for silence is good.

- **Tone:** "mmmmmm" or "aum". The eternal sound of all creation, the basis of all structure. Represents unlimited pure consciousness and yet contains all matter.

- **Gems: amethyst** has the highest vibration of all crystals. It guides you to the infinite and stimulates the crown. **Clear quartz** brings clear light to the mind and soul and helps you to merge with the universe. **Diamonds** are also beneficial for the crown.

- **Essential oils: frankincense** (olibanum) changes your consciousness, cleanses and opens your chakras via the crown; it opens you to God and it is a holy scent. **Lotus** flower is also for the crown but not easily available. Rosewood and lavender may also be used but are not as powerful.

- All **ascended masters** work through here because all is God. **Apply any of the Master Oils on the crown chakra (top of your head) to have a more profound connection to the Masters and harmonize this chakra.**

- **Breathe** into this area, observe the color, feelings and sensations.

- **Look** at a full rose, study it from the centre outwards. (The rose is the flower of highest vibration, symbolic of Christ consciousness).

- **Ask** to have an experience of your God.

- Cover your eyes and ears and make the 'mmmm' tone, then **meditate** while focusing on the crown layers. Especially look at the symbol held in your overself, and draw or make it. Also go to your star or planet, become more familiar with it. Don't overdo it! If you have strange sensations in the head, ease off a bit.

• **Mirror homework:** sit up close to the mirror.* Look at your self intently; then defocus eyes (make them go soft) and ask these questions: "Who am I really? What am I really like?" Then find something beautiful about yourself. Find something exquisite about yourself. Find something vulnerable and humorous about yourself. Can you see joy in your reflection? Can you release all judgement about your face and see it soften? Can you thank your higher self for creating you just the way you are? Do this **at least once** this month. Also just look at yourself in the mirror by candlelight and observe all the different faces that you can see.

---

* **Note**: You may experience other faces or other beings appearing - do not fear, you are in control, just close your eyes and you will return to normal consciousness. The other faces may be some of your own past life faces, or may be spiritual guides there to help you.

EIGHTH - TWELFTH CHAKRAS

I would like to discuss briefly what I see as the Eighth to Twelfth Chakras. I can see that they are beginning to activate more and more in the aura of the individual.

The chakras Eight - Eleven are spinning vortexes of energy situated on the edge of your energy body, your aura. The twelfth chakra is different again. The 8-11 chakras are smaller than the ones associated with the physical body, but are developing over time according to humanity's development. They are being stimulated now, and opening up more, as we move into the twentyfirst century and its new way of living and being.

As individuals wake up to a greater sense of reality there will be more opening and movement of these chakras. They don't necessarily activate in order.

The diagram below shows the position of the Eighth, Ninth and Tenth chakras and how these chakras are connected, not only to each other, but also to the Throat chakra, the Third Eye and the Crown chakra gates.

EIGHTH CHAKRA

As we become more aware the Eighth chakra activates and opens more. It has to open for us to evolve into the 21st Century and the new consciousness.

This chakra is located above the Crown Chakra gates sitting on the edge of the aura, like a spinning cone or vortex of energy with the narrow point inside our aura, and the larger more open end of the cone pointing out towards the world around you.

DIAGRAM 10
Upper chakras connecting to bliss

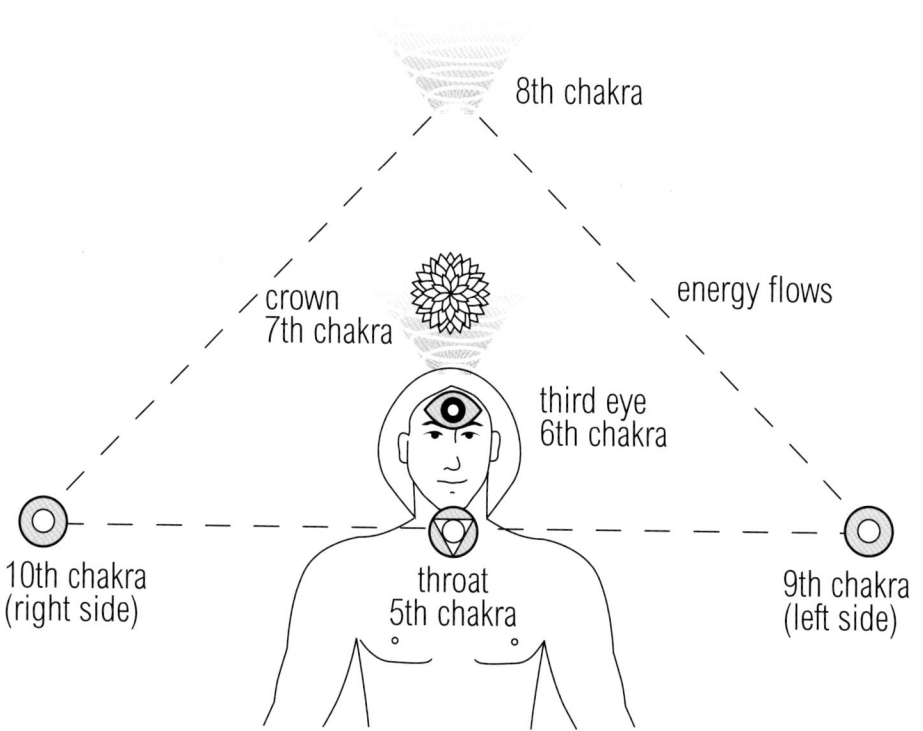

8th chakra

crown
7th chakra

energy flows

third eye
6th chakra

10th chakra
(right side)

throat
5th chakra

9th chakra
(left side)

Upper Chakras

The main function of this chakra is to give us a symbolic understanding of life. It gives us a larger view of life; it is related to archetypes and mythology.

Archetypes are universally recognised themes, images, patterns, stories that provide a symbolic view of our human experience. When this chakra is working, it starts to free you. You get a new perspective on life, your self and others and so on. You gain a clearer and higher perspective and understanding, the bigger picture, and a deeper understanding of your life.

This is the link between the personal consciousness and the higher self (that part of you that cannot fully incarnate). As we move into the Aquarian Age, the archetypes will become more apparent and accessible. They will become more fully understood. (To learn more about archetypes, I suggest you read books by Joseph Campbell or Caroline Myss.)

This chakra has a much finer, faster, higher vibration than the other chakras, it is very sensitive. It connects us to archetypal beings of the universe. Archetypes connect *everyone* on the planet; the same symbols are drawn by children, up to the age of about seven years, in all cultures, and others appear in the ritual or sacred art of all cultures down the ages.

When the Eighth chakra opens, you connect to the universal mind and can receive direct learning. This learning and teaching comes direct from God, not from a human teacher, or a book, or a course; it comes more directly from the spiritual world and your Higher Self. Through this teaching you become more conscious. These archetypes and symbols show up in our dreams and in every day life, are found in movies, art, the people and things around you. When you appreciate the archetypes, it is easier to understand people, and forgive, heal, love and be tolerant of all others, without judgment. You have an inner awareness and knowing.

When this chakra is just opening, a person can go the other extreme and see symbolism in *everything* ... It can be annoying when someone starts to see symbolic meaning in absolutely everything, but they get over it eventually and regain balance. As Freud said, "sometimes a cigar is just a cigar ..."

When you say "I Am" followed by a title or a name, (for example, "I am an artist"), you pull in that IAM energy from the universe, from the collective unconscious. It is very powerful. In doing this you connect to all others who have identified themselves as an artist, and whatever energy they have, whether it be dark and depressed, or divinely inspired, you will pull it down upon you, so to speak. So be very careful, and be very specific. "I am a great, successful, happy and inspired artist" would be better. Deliberately connect to the highest, grandest, most successful energies and positive expression of the archetype that you want to bring in for yourself.

The difference between saying "I feel ..." and "I am ..." is very great. Every time you say to yourself "I am hopeless, weak, a failure ..." you pull that energy in to yourself, from all the people who have ever felt hopeless, weak, and a failure, as it is held in the collective mind of the IAM. What you really mean to say is "I feel hopeless" "I feel weak" etcetera, because the I AM is infinite becoming, whereas a feeling is fleeting and belongs only to you. We all have this feeling of being a failure, at times, but it goes, it is fleeting - feel it, but do not become it.

The colour this chakra vibrates to is a pale **turquoise, aquamarine** colour *plus* gold.

Horus, the Egyptian sun god, relates to this chakra. The Eye of Horus is an ancient symbol peculiar to initiates, and helps to open this chakra. This energy is becoming more important, and will be over the next 2000 years.

The essential oils for this chakra are lavender and rose.

As with the other chakras putting your awareness into this chakra, helps to stimulate it. Have a go!

NINTH CHAKRA

This chakra is located on the left side of the body, about neck and shoulder level, at the edge of the aura. The function of the Ninth chakra is to hold the energy and experience of your past lives.

If this chakra is open, you will be able to know or see or feel aspects of your own past lives. You no longer 'believe' in past lives, you 'know' them. Access to this past can be used as a tool for release and renewal.

This chakra is a vortex or portal to *your* tunnel of time. During the past fifty years it has started to be more active in people, making past life information more accessible.

Any being that is a Guardian of the Threshold is associated with this chakra. For instance, Ascended Master Julian has an energetic connection with the Ninth chakra.

The colour this chakra vibrates to is a rich **indigo** plus gold, and the essential oil which resonates with its nature is patchouli.

The Ninth and Tenth chakras can be stimulated or activated by holding your arm straight out to the side, (to the left, or right) and where your hand is at the edge of your aura, there is the chakra - click with your fingers a few times. It works! Experiment and see what you can sense, if anything happens. Your awareness will come slowly, slowly, - you won't click your fingers at your Ninth chakra and suddenly see lifetimes of passing by on a three dimensional screen - but you may get glimpses, ideas, feelings, even smells or perhaps sensations of hot or cold for example, if you connect to a life where you lived in the desert or in the snowy mountains.

TENTH CHAKRA

The Tenth chakra is on the right side of your aura at the same level as the Ninth chakra. The function of this chakra relates to the future.

This chakra is connected to our Third Eye Chakra, as is the Ninth chakra, so the fine energies of the Third Eye need to be clear somewhat for the Ninth and Tenth chakra to operate. This chakra leads us to the future; it is the gateway to the future for us. It is not that your future is written indelibly for you, but that it is there and the Tenth chakra holds its possibilities for you, your possible futures, the opportunities, the *plan* (it is only the plan, its details are flexible).

It is natural and instinctual for us to want to know our future. It comes from our more primitive times; when we needed to know for our survival when is it going to be hot or cold? Where is the food? Where is the water? What is the weather doing? We needed to 'tune in' for our survival.

Modern technology and communication has closed us down instinctively; we don't have to tune in, we can turn on a radio, watch TV, call a friend, get the weather report. We have stopped using this faculty so it has diminished somewhat. Yet, we all do attempt to prophesy in some way -we call it planning for the future, or 'forward thinking' ... these are ways of projecting current energy into the future; it is the same thing! We just don't feel it in the same way as we used to, nor do we trust it as we used to.

Have you ever experienced a sense or dream or vision or message of some sort about your own future?

Prophets and astrologers as advisors were accepted and acknowledged up until quite recently. St. Augustus was very powerful, and exerted influence against the use of astrology. His reasoning was: how can planets affect people when only God has that power? Then it was said that clairvoyance and prophecy was the work of the devil. This made it dangerous for people to think for themselves and trust in their own natural intuition. Their natural gift and power was taken away, and the church became the repository of all knowledge and all power: the common people were expected to turn to their priest for guidance, which he mediated for them from God, and they lost their direct connection with the Divine; it was forbidden to them.

The risk that you run by consulting a clairvoyant for readings is that you come to rely on that external source rather than developing your own inner knowing. You have to feel it yourself and think for yourself. It's okay to see someone occasionally for guidance or a bit of a kick to get you back on track! But it is not good to rely on someone else to the extent that you regularly sidestep your own growth and development.

You still have to feel what they're saying, and judge whether it's true for you or not. You know that when you realise something and feel something yourself, how much power it has. But if someone else tells you and you don't *feel it,* then you don't connect with it and it doesn't have much power in your life at all.

At any given moment, there are at least ten possible futures open to you. You have free will, free choice. You may have been working on an issue for ten years or ten lifetimes, and when that moment arrives, when you've finally *got* it, something goes 'ping' and all of a sudden the path you were treading is no longer relevant. Lots of new ones open up to you as soon as you get the lesson, and release the karma from the chakra, and you step into your next phase of growth, and onto the next stage of your soul's journey.

Always remember though, knowing the future is not nearly as important as *living today and being in the moment!*

The Tenth chakra, the future chakra is still quite inactive in most people. The Ninth chakra is more easily opened at the moment, although the Tenth chakra will soon start to 'loosen' as we evolve and grow in this the 21st Century.

As with the Ninth chakra, this chakra can be stimulated by clicking your fingers, at arms length, at the spot where the Tenth chakra is situated, at the edge of your aura to your right.

The colour that this chakra vibrates to is **lime green** with gold. A fresh pretty lime green colour is the colour of the future. If you want to bring in a happier future for yourself, wear lime green.

The essential oil to use to stimulate this chakra is, of course, the oil of Lime.

ELEVENTH CHAKRA

The Eleventh chakra is located beneath and between your feet, at the edge of your aura. It is literally in the earth.

The main function of this chakra is Intention: *your intention* as it manifests here on earth, and what motivates you, anchoring that energy into the earth plane of physicality, making it real. This chakra holds the energy so that the intention does not just sit in your brain, and remain an idea, but reaches your feet also, so to speak, and becomes manifest.

The purer your intentions are, the clearer and more connected to earth you are, and the more this chakra is alive. If it is open, your intentions are pure.

This chakra is also connected to the initiation process.

The Eleventh chakra is a very rich **chocolate brown** with gold in colour. Wearing this colour will help you to connect and open this chakra.

The essential oil for this chakra is clary sage.

Putting your attention into this chakra helps it to awaken more fully, so try to locate it just below your feet in your mind's eye, or sense it.

TWELFTH CHAKRA

The Twelfth Chakra is you. This chakra quite different to the other chakras, as it is the cosmic level of your whole being. To the more highly evolved universal beings looking at us from that level, we are each like chakras in the universe! We each look like a spinning vortex of energy, a soul chakra. So this twelfth chakra is the whole, complete you, glowing a-light in the Cosmos. It is your light in the universe, and is inter-dimensional.

The colour of this chakra is shining shimmering gold. Wearing **gold** (the element) helps your whole being. When you are gold and all your chakras are clear and vibrating with the pulse of the Divine, you know who you are, you know your place in the universe; your "I AM" is fully developed. You become IAMTHATIAM.

KUNDALINI

The kundalini force is really a mystery, although yogis have been teaching about it for thousands of years. Yogis have devoted many scriptures to exercises on how to raise your kundalini. These teachings have been preparing us for this time.

In the coming age of Aquarius, kundalini will be talked about a great deal; like the word 'chakra', it will be in common use, especially over the next 100-200 years, and after that it will be accepted as a normal part of human development. (When any word or concept comes into the common language it is an indication of the expanding awareness or consciousness of that concept at that time.)

'Kund' means to burn. 'Kunda' means a bowl, or vessel. 'Kundala' means a coil or spiral or ring. '-ini' is a feminine word ending. So it is a feminine burning force contained in a coiled spiral in a bowl-shaped vessel. It is located at the base of the spine, the coccyx. This feminine creative force sleeps in the sacred bowl within you, and when it gradually wakens within it feels like streams of fire, ascending and descending the spine. (Jacobs Ladder is a symbolic biblical reference to kundalini).

The kundalini is a God-force - a feminine God force, often called the Serpent fire, Shakti. This is why the kundalini energy will be activated more fully in both males and females, over the next century, to bring in more fully the feminine powers and combine them with the masculine power.

When the chakras start to open, the kundalini starts to rise. Ultimately, it will travel from the base of the spine up to the crown chakra, (at which time you will be enlightened!). The kundalini starts to rise as your focus turns inward, when you are no longer so concerned with the outside world. Because it is such a powerful force, your chakras need to be balanced and in good health, otherwise it can be destructive. It should not be woken before time, which is why the ancient yogis devoted so much energy to preparation and to controlling it, so that they could raise it without destroying themselves.

Generally, it starts to move naturally within a person sometime between 38 and about 50 years of age. (This is assuming that they are in reasonably good health.) Emotional and physical structures have to be very strong and healthy in the individual first, before there is any movement of the kundalini. Sometimes people do not take the opportunities for growth that they are presented with during their life journey, sometimes they stagnate, and this means that they will have no experience of the God-fire rising in this incarnation.

At 35 years old, you are the sum total of all your incarnations; until then life is training you and you are 'remembering' who you are. This is a very important anniversary because at around this time we are required to make a life-changing decision, which usually involves taking a big risk. Something like: moving countries; having a baby; getting divorced; starting a business; embracing spiritual truth. If we dare to say "Yes" to the challenge, our life expands and our real purpose, that for which we incarnated, starts to come more fully into being. Before that we are training ourselves to be ready for our life purpose. Acting on the challenge prepares the person for the possibility of the kundalini rising subsequently.

Note: Occasionally, the kundalini can be active in people much younger that this, and indeed it will start happening earlier in life as we move forward into the new energy. If it is active in younger people to some degree they usually have a strong 'destiny', a purpose that will not let them go - maybe Mozart was an example of this!

There seem to be two ways of evolving: one is the gradual path, where you slowly and steadily progress. The other is more sporadic and explosive, where you blast up then hit a plateau for a while, then blast up another level, plateau again, and so on. It is the same with kundalini. In some it forges the path up the spine very slowly, gradually and gently. In others it blasts through the chakras destroying everything blocked in its path. This is why the lower chakras need to be strong, this is your foundation upon which you are built and if you are not 'master' of the lower three chakras (first, second and third) then the kundalini will remain asleep within you.

When the kundalini force starts rising within you it feels like 'mini orgasms' flooding up your spine; if it reaches the head, you feel a very warm loving feeling, it is delicious! You cannot recreate it within yourself - you must not force it, or grasp at it; just observe its flowing.

As well as personal kundalini, there is also solar kundalini energy (from the sun) and earth kundalini energy. Generally, because the kundalini force is not very active in people, the solar and earth kundalini forces just go around you, bypassing you but still connecting with each other. (See the diagram below.) When it starts to move in you, the solar kundalini links up to the earth kundalini through **your body**, you become a conductor of this energy, and are truly actively participating in the cosmos. (In the tarot, the Magician Card depicts this, with one of his arms reaching up to the sky and the other pointing into the earth - to be able to conduct these cosmic forces through you is to have real magical power.) To conduct this power, you need to prepare and be strong to hold it.

Eventually, we will also be able to link up other, stellar, kundalini - so we will truly become connected to the sun, the earth, the stars, … everything.

This level of consciousness steadily held, brings enlightenment, freedom and release.

When the power is out of control, or misdirected, raising the kundalini can cause mental illness and sexual depravity. When it moves as it is meant to, it feels like a spinal glow; all the chakras will be refined and glow with a higher light.

Kundalini energy may intensify any existing back pain, making the spine feel raw at times. It can feel like electricity in the body, an electric current running through you that you can't always turn off. It heightens all your senses, things seem to become multi-dimensional, and you can remain conscious even while you sleep.

Your soul and Higher Self will conduct much of your preparation while you sleep. The spinal channels are prepared for a long time while asleep, with maybe years of clearing going on. When you first start to

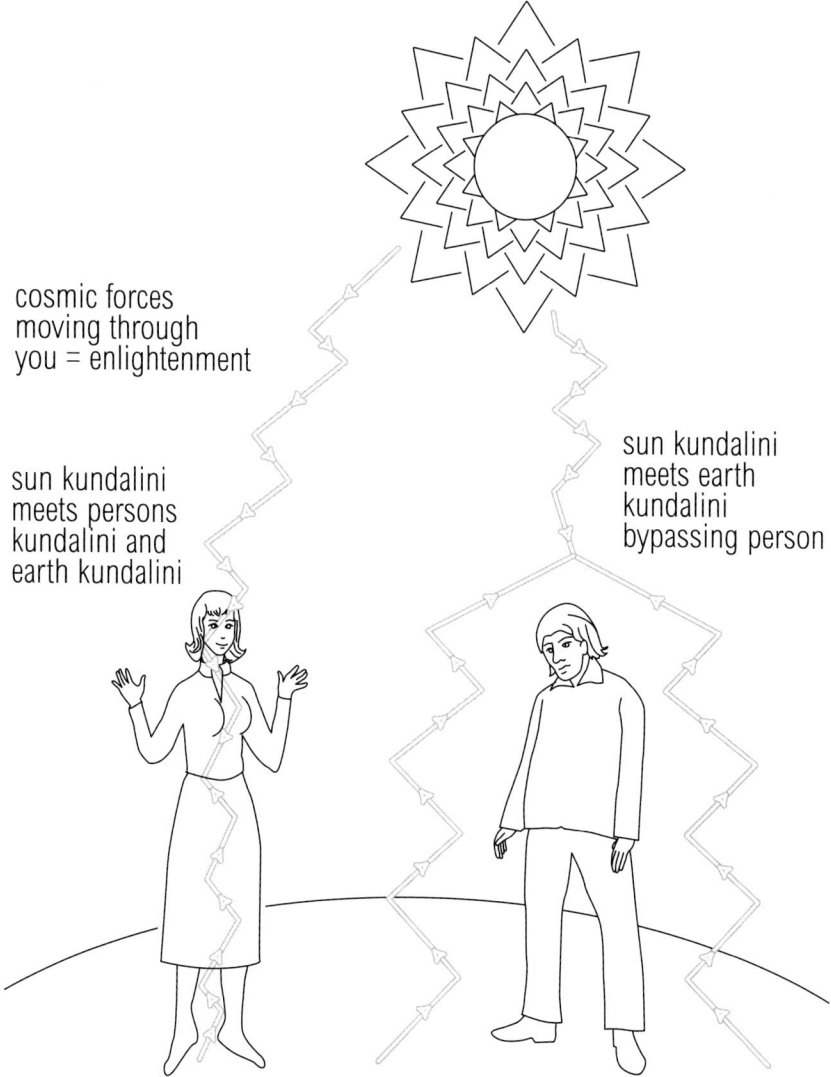

cosmic forces
moving through
you = enlightenment

sun kundalini
meets persons
kundalini and
earth kundalini

sun kundalini
meets earth
kundalini
bypassing person

Sun/Earth Kundalini

become conscious of the kundalini energy moving, you may feel dizziness, or feel as though you are a long way away, or numb. Sometimes it seems like everything external has become two dimensional, flat, meaningless, but paradoxically, your *inner* life is becoming more rich, more alive. Your intuition is heightened, yet you're not particularly interested in the world around you. You might also feel itchy, twitchy, tingling, shaking, fluttery, vibrations in the spine or your whole body.

Remember that whenever you hit a new dimension of reality, you will take time to adjust, and this often results in dizziness; this is a physical expression of a new spiritual reality.*

Note: **Nicotine** creates a barrier to its flow. **Alcohol** stimulates it, but in the **wrong** direction, (it 'blows out' usually sideways), which can then create violence or rage within the person. This can happen if there is a misuse or abuse of alcohol, that is, consuming too much over long periods. (One or two alcoholic drinks per day is okay, and is not enough to cause any 'damage' to the kundalini force).

ORIGINAL GRIEF

The most common block to the kundalini rising is unreleased grief, (held in the third chakra, the solar plexus), from this and, or, other lifetimes. When the kundalini energy hits the third chakra it activates the grief, and generally the *"it's not ok to be me"* pattern comes up. You might feel the grief for a long time, bringing up the tears (which cleanse the chakras), and it may seem that the grief is endless - this is not so. It is a positive thing, because when you have released the grief it is gone forever, and then the kundalini will travel up, and your life will be changed for the better!

This type of deep grieving takes you back to what I call the **'original grief'**. That is, the first time you felt this deep and extraordinary grief was when you had the experience of being 'cut off' from God, from the heavens, from spirit; in other words, from your real home.

---

* As always, check with your medical practitioner if you experience any dizziness, or other complaints in the physical - never assume the condition is only spiritual. Even if the cause is spiritual, if it has manifested itself in the physical body, then the physical needs to be healed by physical means as well as spiritual.

We are reminded of this 'cutting' every time we incarnate, as the umbilical cord is cut separating us from the Mother (womb-heaven) and we have to leave Mother (God) once again and learn to travel alone. Once this level of grief is released from you, you then realize and know on the deepest soul level that you are not disconnected from your 'home' or from 'god' and that in fact the divine lives within you as part of you. You are never alone when you have got **you**.

KUNDALINI BREATH

Sometimes called 'breath of fire' this is designed to raise the kundalini. It has been used for thousands of years by the yogis. It is also very purifying for the body, accelerating release of toxins and old energy via the breath.

It is important to drink plenty of water after practising this. Start by only doing it for half a minute or so, work up to longer stretches: do not force it to move into particular parts of the body. Observe where it travels. Always rest for a few minutes afterwards, and then do the earth connection exercise or some other grounding exercise.

Technique: Sit forward on the edge of the chair or cross-legged on the floor, so your spine is upright, (do not slouch or else the energy cannot travel upwards).

Breathe from the belly. Expand the lower belly as you breathe in, contract the belly when you breathe out through your mouth. This is the natural rhythm of breathing. Now speed up the process...you are aiming for about 3 breaths per second. It is a pumping action from the belly muscles. Do this for about **half a minute** or 90 fast breaths. Then take a full breath in, hold the breath as long as is comfortable, with your chin tucked in towards your neck or collar bone and your spine upright, also contract all your pelvic floor muscles and perineum as you are holding your breath. (This is to keep the energy moving along the spine rather than spinning out in the aura.) Breathe out and relax everything, observing what is happening in your body. Rest for a minute and then repeat this process. Gradually work up to doing this for a minute at a time. Do this once a day, in the morning, every day for at least month.

CONCLUSION

What do you need to live a happy life?

Life's challenges and experiences develop the chakras. Life will present you with all the challenges and adventures that you need for your growth and fulfilment - what you do with these opportunities is your choice.

Evolution is a natural process; it happens anyway. It doesn't have to be difficult. All around us are forces and energies that are there to facilitate this for you: your evolution, your growth, success, healing, joy and fulfilment. We have talked about the chakras and the many simple things you can do to nourish them. Many of these things are naturally occurring in our daily lives, so nature heals us without us being aware of it; the colours, the fragrance, the beauty of nature and of life send us the vibrations that we need to heal or harmonize an unhappy chakra. The clear sunshine thrills all the chakras, the trees and flowers soothe and encourage us, the blue sky, the ocean's forces expand the chakras instantly. It is all around us! Having eyes open to see this, having awareness of it all, increases its value to you.

The extraordinary phenomenon we call Crop Circles is another example of how the spiritual world and the natural world work together to 'fast forward' our evolution. The unbelievable and ingenious symbolic language (the language of the gods) that appears in the fields of corn (and other crops) is imprinting not only upon the earth and her energy field, on her etheric body (which in turn has an effect upon all that takes its sustenance from the earth) but also upon *our* etheric body and consciousness. Some of these remarkable crop circles (the genuine ones) are 'sent' to work directly upon a particular chakra in humans, whether we are conscious of it or not. Remember that chakras are spiritual centres that not only link to each other but also act as a bridge between the fine spiritual energies and the more dense physical energies in us.

You are a remarkable human being. Both physical and spiritual.

You are You, much loved; *never* forget this.

GLOSSARY OF TERMS

Akashic Records

The Akasha is at the etheric level of existence. Each of us has, in the Akasha, a unique place where a vibrational record is kept of everything we have been, done or said, in all of our existence, in this physical life and others. All our energetic actions are imprinted on the ether at our special point, like a thumbprint on wax, and these go to make up our personal Akashic record. For those who can see this realm, the Akashic records are visible, readable.

Angels/Angelic Realm

Angels are beings whose energy is far higher and faster than ours. They exist primarily in the Astral plane, though they can make themselves felt in the etheric and physical levels; to us, their energy feels thrilling, and may be physically exhausting. Generally speaking, Angelic beings have never been human; they have never incarnated. There is a hierarchy of Angels, Archangels, Mights, Powers, Dominions etc. and each have their own mission. Angels help to connect us with the higher dimensions, and in turn we help to connect them with the physical world.

Ascended Masters

Ascended Masters are highly evolved beings who have undergone a sequence of initiation as incarnate human beings. They have all achieved a level of spiritual development advanced enough to be freed from the need to incarnate again. The Masters all work towards the realisation of perfection, and some work closely with humanity. Each Master has a personality and energy exclusively their own, and it is possible for us to have a very personal relationship with many of them. Some, for example, Lady Portia, St Germain, Kuthumi, are working very closely with humanity at present to bring in the energy of the New Age.

Astral Body

We are made up of a number of intersecting, overlapping energy bodies. Our physical body is the slowest vibration, and we can see this in the physical world. Our Astral Body is of a much higher, faster vibration, and extends beyond our physical body by about thirty centimetres or more. It can detach from the physical body and travel independently, (when we sleep perhaps), through the astral plane. It enables physical movement, so that, for example, when alcohol affects the alignment of the astral body with the physical, our control over our physical movements is impaired; if we drink too much, the astral is unhooked to the extent that we pass out. The astral body also gives us the ability to be conscious - to have a level of consciousness.

Atlantis

Atlantis was an age in our development, about 13,000 to 20,000 years ago. In the Atlantean Age we had developed to a very advanced technical level; we had highly developed psychic ability and were very skilled in the use of energy and light. In Atlantis these powers were abused by some; genetic monstrosities were created and a psychic war was waged. As a defence, our third eyes were closed; the civilisation collapsed. This struggle is being re-enacted in our time, as we have the opportunity to assimilate our power and apply it without abusing Nature or each other.

Aura

Aura is a general term for the group of energy bodies which enclose our physical body. It extends, generally, anything from a few centimetres from the body to a metre or more. It can be seen as a cloud of light of varying colours around the physical, and the state of the individual and the individual's soul is reflected in its shape and colours. (See Diagram.)

Chakra

Chakra means, literally, wheel; the chakras in our energy bodies are centres of energy, nodes in the circuits of energy which constitute our

body, and when we are healthy and well balanced, these centres spin. There are seven major chakras located on the physical body and four others within the aura, near the body. Each chakra has a nature of its own, and is related to particular physical (and other) organs and functions.

Christ Consciousness

Christ Consciousness is the energy, awareness, which Jesus the Christ, and Buddha, embodied. It is the energy which we are at this time enabling to return to earth in each one of us. It is a Light of Love, a White Light which we can draw into our own energy field, and which raises the vibration of all we come in contact with. It is Pure Love, the energy of our time, in which we are aware of our at-one-ness with all things.

Consciousness

Consciousness is a level of awareness; it may exist on many levels, but is associated with higher levels of existence; it gives us the ability to observe ourself, to learn and evolve as spiritual beings.

Dimensions

Dimensions are levels of existence, and the 'higher' the dimension, the more complex the existence it may support. For example, in two dimensional reality, a sphere looks like a circle, and in one dimension it looks like a dot: to see the sphere, you must have access to three dimensions, and to see a ball bounce you must access four (space and time). This book exists in three dimensions - our experience as we work with this book certainly exists in four dimensions, (space and time), and may also take us into higher dimensions, where Love, or Bliss exists.

Energy Body

All things are made up of energy - as modern physics would have it, 'intelligent energy', energy with a purpose. We are made up of a number of overlapping patterns of intelligent energy, overlapping

energy bodies, and each energy body is different, and has different qualities. (See the sections on Aura, Astral Body, and Etheric Body.)

Ensouled

We are 'ensouled' when we connect with the Divine while we are in our physical bodies: we are wells into which the Light pours. Our current task is to be able to connect with higher realities without leaving our bodies in order to do it: in times past spiritual practice has taught people how to go to other dimensions (by meditation and so on), but now we are learning to accept and hold the Light within us while still being active in the physical world.

Ego Boundaries

Ego is a part of your identity which enables you to feel individual, and to identify yourself as distinct from other people. In order to feel secure and independent as an individual, we need to establish firm ego boundaries. These boundaries are elastic in that we can permit some people to come closer to us than others without feeling threatened. Most people are aware of the existence of their ego boundaries, especially when they meet someone who crosses them against their will. Ideally our ego boundaries are strong and flexible.

Electro-magnetic Field

This is the space which is created by the interaction of electric and magnetic forces - light is an electro-magnetic energy; all energy which comes from matter is electro-magnetic. It is also, incidentally, the energy which is used to power your car engine, and operate your dimmer switch! The electro-magnetic field contains vast regions of visible and invisible energy which we have barely begun to understand.

Etheric Body

The etheric body is an energy body which is very similar to the physical body; it is 'lighter', of a slightly higher vibration, and is not usually visible. It extends slightly beyond the physical body, and

provides a 'template' for it. Everything which has an etheric body is somehow 'alive'. (See the entry for Energy Body.)

Great Love

The 'great love' is a love which is beyond and above a personal love, and comes upon us, inhabits us, with a power and conviction that are undeniable, exquisite, perfect; the great love is that feeling that you hold when you are connected to your Divine purpose, and are following it. It is not like any other love.

Higher Self

The Higher Self is the term we give to describe that part of our self which is enduring, which is beyond our everyday concerns, and untroubled by our human emotions: it speaks to us with a 'still small voice of calm' and an absolute clarity. It is our true self, knows us and the needs of spirit clearly and kindly, and it is active in arranging to bring us the life experience which we need 'for our highest good'. It never speaks negatively of us or others.

IAMNESS

Your Iamness is the pure essential nature of You. It is the core of your being, towards which you are evolving, and which you always are. As you proceed on your spiritual path, your Iamness is what you seek, what guides you and what gives you strength; it is the You that you constantly strive towards. Merging with your Iamness is the highest spiritual act you can perform. In other words it is your Christ-self, the divine within you.

Manifest

Manifest means to make real, to realise. It is a spiritual law that 'form follows thought', which is to say that what we believe, or dwell on, we manifest.

New Consciousness

At this time in the evolution of humanity there is a shift in consciousness imminent; a new awareness, a new consciousness, will become the norm for humanity as a whole. In the new consciousness we will be able to hold the energy of spirit while functioning in the physical world; we will be able to carry our spiritual connection around with us, instead of having to retreat from everyday life in order to access it.

New Age

The New Age is a phrase used to describe the next major stage in the evolution of humanity, in which the 'new consciousness' becomes commonplace (eventually!). We are at the threshold of the New Age now, and much of the upheaval in the world, and the rapid changes in it over the last hundred years, are indications that we are in a time of great transition.

Overlighting

It sometimes happens that the energy of a Master, or Angel, can descend around and over us, so that we experience them almost as though we are the same; this is called overlighting. The Master lowers their energy over us (like a lampshade over a lamp) and enables us to have a direct experience of them, their energy, their understanding. Overlighting is not unconscious, is not 'channelling', and is not at all like being 'possessed'.

Portal

Literally, a portal is a doorway; here we use it to describe a connection between worlds, through which energies can travel. A portal is a point (or time) of access, an opportunity; an opportunity to access another world, another energy, to transform.

Ritual

Ritual is a way of behaving, or an action, or sequence of actions, which have come to have power and meaning beyond the ordinary. A

ritual action may be simple or complex; what is important is that we have invested special meaning to it, it becomes symbolic and so carries power. For example, if we customarily light a candle before we pray, the act of lighting a candle becomes a simple ritual which calls up the attitude of prayer, invites the higher beings which attend us when we pray, and creates the right atmosphere for us, wherever we are.

Soul

Soul is that aspect of ourselves which is evolving; which we take from one life to another, perfecting it (or not) through our experience as incarnated beings. (See Spirit)

Spirit

We each have a Spirit, or spiritual aspect of ourselves, which is perfect at all times; unlike our Soul aspect, our Spiritual self is always at its highest level of expression, and is not perfected through experience. When we talk of Spirit we talk of a level of being which is permanent, constant, and pure. Spirit is also used to denote that level of being, or energy, which is absolute and perfect: we talk of Spirit as being a perfect moving force behind the urge to Bliss, or toward a higher level of existence.

Spiritual

When we describe something here as spiritual, we mean to say that it is moved by Spirit, or of spirit; it is to do with an urge to evolve towards the highest, finest vibration of existence.

Will

Will is desire which leads to action. On a personal level, when you truly will something, that has great force and power to achieve, or manifest; it is far more than simply 'wanting'. Your Higher Self wills your spiritual evolution, and perfectly organises your experience in the world towards that end. To wield our Will-power in a positive way is not selfish, and one of the lessons we all must learn; when it is negatively used it acts against other people (as bullying and violence, for example) and to our detriment.

FAQS

What is karma?

Karma is the Law of Cause and Effect; "every action generates a force of energy that returns to us in like kind"; that is, whatever you sow, so you shall reap. Karma is a quality of time, and is about understanding. The Law of Forgiveness is above the Law of Karma, and is a path out of difficult karma, and clears karmic debts.

What is reincarnation?

Reincarnation means 're-entry into the flesh'. The essence of your being (your soul) re-enters a new physical body to learn, experience, explore and evolve as a human being. We are reborn into new bodies in many different lifetimes to have varied expressions of our being (so that eventually our being becomes whole).

What is the difference between Soul and Spirit?

As the physical body is a vehicle for your soul, the soul is a vehicle for your spirit. The soul is evolving so is not perfect yet, the spirit is like a river of light flowing through your soul but it is not attached to the physical body. (See the Glossary)

Are there more souls being created?

Yes, there are new souls being created as other souls ascend (complete their earthly lives). People are reincarnating more quickly than they used to, so there are more people on earth at this time in evolution.

What is initiation?

Through arduous training an initiation can occur, which means you reach a higher level of consciousness and forever change your reality. There are many levels of initiation. In the ancient days we were initiated through the temples (if we were ready); today, life initiates us. Many people have not attained the 'First Degree' of initiation yet; whereas an Ascended Master (see Masters of the Universe) is at least a Fifth Degree initiate.

What is meant by different dimensions?

We are all aware that we live in the four dimensions of time and space, and we are aware of the dimensions below this one, the first, second and third. There are nine dimensions altogether that we can experience as humans. Each dimension has its own vibration, and is a level of existence, a level of reality.

What are the Rays?

This is a terms used to describe a level of consciousness. There are 12 main rays, but there are many more. Most people in the western world at the moment exist on the fourth Ray which is the Ray of "Harmony through Conflict".

What are archetypes?

'Archetype' is a Jungian term used to describe a common theme or energy that arises from the 'collective unconscious'. For example, the warrior, wicked witch, networker, nun, victim (and so on) are all archetypes, and their nature and characteristics are immediately obvious to us.

Can we come back as a fly if we have been 'bad' in a lifetime?

My understanding is that we can't come back as a member of a different 'kingdom', for example as an animal, or a plant. We can however, stultify, which means we can stagnate or 'fall back' in our own personal evolution as a human soul. If we have been 'bad' then we incur karma that, at some stage when the soul is strong enough, will have to be harmonized.

Do we have a soul mate?

Yes, though I prefer the term soul friends. These are souls (people) who are in our soul stream, who have perhaps followed a similar path to us and who we have incarnated with many times in different roles. They are on a similar level of consciousness to us so we feel deeply connected to them and we know they truly understand us. It is a soul bond, which can be with a male or female.

Have we been both male and female in our lives?

Yes, the soul is neither male nor female, black or white, Jewish, Christian, Buddhist, pauper or king. It is itself having the experience of being male or female, Jewish, wealthy or poor for its own development.

Other books and products from Cobolt Connection P/L:

- **Bliss Book - Six Steps to a New Consciousness**
- **Ascended Masters Book - Volume I**
- **Ascended Masters Book - Volume II**
- **Written information on other metaphysical subjects.**
- **CDs of guided meditation with different Ascended Masters.**
- **Master oils**
- **Meditation symbols**

These products are available for purchase via the website www.cobolt.com.au or by contacting:

Cobolt Connection Pty Ltd
Suite 1102/1 Queens Road
Melbourne, Victoria
Australia 3004

Phone: (03) 9863 9333
Fax: (03) 9863 9336

Email: info@cobolt.com.au
Website: www.cobolt.com.au